DYNAMIC
YOUTH
SERVICES

through Outcome-Based
Planning and Evaluation

Eliza T. Dresang

Melissa Gross

Leslie Edmonds Holt

Foreword by Virginia Walter

American Library Association
Chicago 2006

While extensive effort has gone into ensuring the reliability of information appearing in this book, the publisher makes no warranty, express or implied, on the accuracy or reliability of the information, and does not assume and hereby disclaims any liability to any person for any loss or damage caused by errors or omissions in this publication.

Printed on 50-pound white offset, a pH-neutral stock, and bound in 10-point coated cover stock by McNaughton & Gunn.

The paper used in this publication meets the minimum requirements of American National Standard for Information Sciences—Permanence of Paper for Printed Library Materials, ANSI Z39.48-1992. ∞

Library of Congress Cataloging-in-Publication Data
Dresang, Eliza T.
      Dynamic youth services through outcome-based planning and evaluation / Eliza T. Dresang, Melissa Gross, Leslie Edmonds Holt ; foreword by Virginia Walter.
         p.   cm.
      Includes bibliographical references and index.
      ISBN 0-8389-0918-3
      1. Children's libraries—Administration. 2. Young adults' libraries—Administration.
3. Children's libraries—Planning. 4. Young adults' libraries—Planning. 5. Children's
libraries—Evaluation. 6. Young adults' libraries—Evaluation. 7. Children's
libraries—Activity programs. 8. Young adults' libraries—Activity programs. 9. Library
planning—United States—Case studies. I. Gross, Melissa. II. Holt, Leslie Edmonds.
III. Title.
      Z718.1.D68 2006
      025.197625—dc22   2006007487

ISBN-10: 0-8389-0918-3
ISBN-13: 978-0-8389-0918-8

Printed in the United States of America

10   09   08   07   06   5   4   3   2   1

CONTENTS

FOREWORD

For the past five years, I have been inspired by an anecdote about the traditional greeting used by Masai warriors. As the story goes, when one warrior sees another warrior, he says, "How are the children?" The other warrior responds, "All the children are well." I have used this story often to communicate to children's librarians the outcome we should all be striving for. Now Eliza Dresang, Melissa Gross, and Leslie Holt have given us some tools for saying with much more confidence and validity, "All the children are well."

As the authors of this groundbreaking book acknowledge, for years I have been urging youth services librarians to use the tools of outcome evaluation in their work for all of the reasons given in this work. We have always had good intentions, but good intentions are, sadly, not enough. If we are going to be effective advocates for excellent library services for children, we must demonstrate the results of those services. Fortunately, our services *do* produce important outcomes for kids; Dresang, Gross, and Holt tell us how to document those outcomes and tell the good news that libraries change young lives for the better.

Even more important, this book presents us with a whole new paradigm for planning. In the past, evaluation came at the end of the planning process, enabling us to see if we met some target objectives. All too often the evaluation and even the setting of targets came almost as an afterthought. In fact, I have occasionally been asked to conduct outcome-based evaluations for services or programs that had not identified outcomes up front. Here the challenge was to identify what outcomes, if any, had been achieved by the program or service.

How much more sense it makes, as this book counsels us, to *start* with the desired outcomes, based on market research and community analysis, then work backward and design the service or program that will achieve the outcome in question and design an evaluation strategy to see if we meet the target. Summer reading programs are an interesting object lesson. Librarians have been providing summer reading programs for at least one hundred years, and the design of these programs has changed little. Maybe summer reading programs would look very different if we started by asking what outcomes we wanted them to achieve.

The kind of research required to do good outcome-based evaluation is a little more rigorous or complex than that required for simple output measurement, but this book provides us with a good refresher course on basic research methods and walks us through the process step by step. The examples from the St. Louis Public Library, where this model for planning and evaluation was developed, are vivid and inspiring. Readers should come away from this book thinking, "If they could do it, so could I."

When I meet another good youth services librarian in the future, perhaps in the aisles of the exhibit floor at an ALA conference, I plan to say, "How are the children?" And he or she will respond, "All the children are well—and I have the outcome evaluation data to prove it."

Virginia Walter
University of California, Los Angeles
November 2005

ACKNOWLEDGMENTS

Developing the CATE outcome-based planning and evaluation (OBPE) model would not have been possible without the support of the Institute of Museum and Library Services in the form of a national leadership grant to the St. Louis Public Library with a subcontract to Florida State University. With this grant, the library and university were able to develop Project CATE, provide outcome-based programs and services to library users, and develop the planning and evaluation model on which this book is based.

We thank the leadership of the Association for Library Service to Children (ALSC), who allowed us the opportunity to introduce Project CATE and the CATE OBPE model at the ALSC regional leadership conference held in St. Louis in October 2002. Interaction with the participants permitted us to improve and shape the OBPE model and disseminate what we had learned about children, computers, and libraries. Special thanks go to ALSC president Cynthia Richey, who asked us to plan and deliver her President's Program, "Myths and Realities: Kids, Technology, and Outcomes in the Public Library," in June 2004 to the ALSC membership, sharing further our findings about the CATE OBPE model and children and technology.

Heartfelt thanks goes to the staff of the St. Louis Public Library. Their flexibility, willingness to try new approaches, and patience as we figured out how to develop new programs for upper elementary and middle school students were essential for the success of Project CATE and the trial of the CATE OBPE model. Particular thanks go to Patty Carleton, Director of Youth Services, and to all her youth services staff who worked directly on the project. Special thanks to Glen Holt, the retired executive director of the St. Louis Public Library, who put us up to writing the grant, urged us forward at every turn, and fostered the receptive and innovative library environment that made our work possible.

We are thankful too for the cooperation and participation of St. Louis library users. Children, parents, teachers, and others answered our questions, told us when we were on course and when we were off base. This willingness helped us create outcomes and then use them to plan and evaluate programs and services. Without this help we would not have learned so much about how to use outcomes.

Consistent and important support also came to the project from the Florida State University College of Information. The encouragement and support of Dean Jane Robbins and numerous other faculty, staff, and students made the effort possible. Special thanks go to Charles R. McClure, Francis Eppes Professor and Director of the Information Use Management and Policy Institute in the College of Information, who listened to our idea of the outcome-based planning and evaluation model and said "Draw it," and to John Carlo Bertot, Professor and Associate Director of the Information Use Management and Policy Institute, who gave us the first opportunity to write about the model in *Evaluating Networked Information Services* (McClure and Bertot 2001).

Finally, we thank Laura Pelehach, our editor at American Library Association, who attended our talk at the Seattle Public Library Association Conference in January 2004 and said "Wouldn't you like to write a book?" She has stood behind us throughout the process, always encouraging us and responding promptly to our questions. Without her, this book would not be.

Eliza T. Dresang
Melissa Gross
Leslie E. Holt

INTRODUCTION

From Seattle to Miami, from Bangor to San Diego, anyone picking up this book will find both an informative framework and specific how-to-do-it tips for planning and evaluating dynamic public library youth services. The size of the library does not matter. The size of the program does not matter. The nature of the service does not matter. The age of the young users does not matter. The following chapters provide a variety of planning and evaluation options for all types of program and service development. The outcome-based planning and evaluation (OBPE) model introduced, called the CATE OBPE model, can be applied to the planning and evaluation of any public library program or service, but in this book focus is on its application to youth. For our purposes, young users are children and young adults from birth through age eighteen or graduation from high school, whichever comes first. The CATE OBPE model helps librarians determine what young users and those interested in youth want the results of library programs and services in which they participate to be, to plan for the desired results, and to evaluate how well they are achieved.

Our main objective in this book is to share what this model is like and why, when, and how to use it—with the necessary background to make it easy to understand and apply to any youth program or service. The model was developed to make straightforward the recommended OBPE process. A flowchart of the CATE OBPE model appears here and throughout the book. We advise readers to get familiar with it, since we mention it many times. At this point, it is not important to focus on the four phases (Gathering Information, Determining

Outcomes, Developing Programs and Services, and Conducting Evaluations) or to try to figure out the exact relationships the various arrows represent. It is, however, important to realize that the model is not linear (one-directional, with Phase I finished, then Phase II completed, and so forth) but interactive, with various phases in operation at any given time. All of this will make sense by the end of the book. For now, just glance at the flowchart and wait for further information.

An important aspect of the CATE OBPE model resides in the words "outcome-based." Outcome, in this book, is the change in attitude, behavior, skill, knowledge, or status that occurs for users after a purposeful action on the part of the library and library staff. Not so long ago, concern about the outcome or impact of services in a public library setting was not part of the formal planning process. But times have changed. Librarians have come to realize that planning based on specific impacts deemed important to library users (and non-users) provides an excellent way to improve library services.

On a more pragmatic note, federal and many state and local agencies now require demonstrated outcomes from libraries requesting funding. Much more about the purpose, procedures, and value of outcome-based planning and evaluation is described throughout the book.

The Story behind the CATE OBPE Model

The CATE OBPE model was developed and tested as a joint research and demonstration project of the Florida State University College of Information and the St. Louis Public Library. The collaboration, called Project CATE, was funded by a grant from the Institute for Museum and Library Services, and we three authors were the project's co-principal investigators: Eliza T. Dresang and Melissa Gross, faculty members at Florida State (both with public library experience), and Leslie Edmonds Holt, director of youth services for the St. Louis Public Library (with university research experience)—all longtime professional colleagues.

The three of us were interested in outcome-based planning and evaluation because it seemed to make good sense and because government funding agencies required it. Dresang and Gross (2001, 28) had developed a prototype of an OBPE model but needed somewhere to test it. The St. Louis Public Library was engaged in a comprehensive planning process regarding youth and technology and wanted to use an outcome-based process. Enhancing this perfect match of needs and interests were Dresang's and Gross's desire to know more about children's

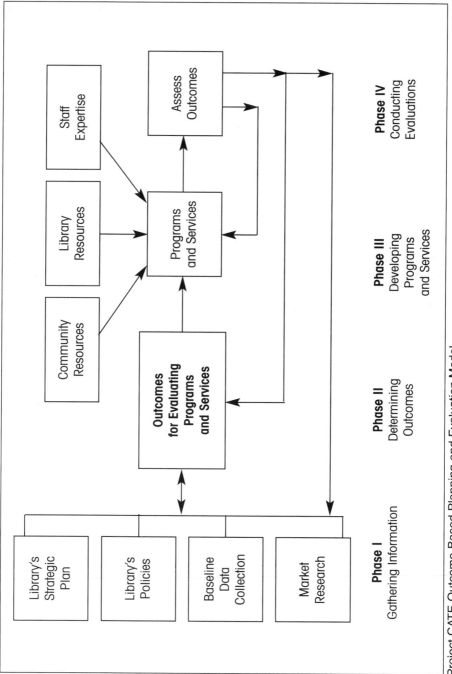

Project CATE Outcome-Based Planning and Evaluation Model

use of technology in a public library setting and their preference to apply the model to this issue. Process and content came together like hand and glove.

What does CATE stand for? It literally stands for Children's Access to and Use of Technology Evaluation. But, as many acronyms tend to do, this one took on a more generalized meaning. In this book, CATE does not refer to an evaluation only of children's technology use but rather denotes the specific outcome-based planning and evaluation model described here, which might be applied to a variety of subjects.

Why the St. Louis Public Library Was a Good Place to Apply the Model

A prime reason for locating the CATE OBPE model's first application in the St. Louis Public Library was the library's long history of youth involvement; surveying young people and inviting them to participate in focus groups were not new to this library environment. That was the plus on the planning and evaluation side.

The St. Louis Public Library was also a good place to study young people's use of technology. It had been the first Gates Learning Foundation Library as well as an e-rate recipient (of government funds for Internet access). The library was also a pioneer among public libraries in realizing the need to evaluate the use of technology by youth in ways that would be proactive and ensure that the city's youth received maximum benefits from the technology the library was able to provide. The library staff and all its stakeholders stood to benefit by the project.

Much had been said in the waning years of the twentieth century about the digital divide, the difference between technology haves and have-nots. Both the Florida State University researchers and the St. Louis library staff wondered whether the recent, rapid, and massive infusion of technology had truly reduced the digital divide, common among urban and minority youth, both prominent among the library clientele. Although the application of the model was the primary focus of the project, many valuable lessons were learned about youth, technology, and the planning environment. For those who are interested, some of the results from the technology study are found in appendix B, the Project CATE Summary Report.

A Few Facts about St. Louis and Its Library

Just as this book is not *about* youth and technology, it is not *about* St. Louis or the St. Louis Public Library. Still, examples scattered throughout the book refer to the application of the CATE OBPE model in studying young peoples' use of technology in St. Louis and the library, so it seems wise to acquaint readers with the context of these illustrations at the time they occurred.

In the years of Project CATE (2001–2003), the St. Louis Public Library was a sixteen-branch library system that served 340,000 people, with an annual budget of $17 million, 1,622,000 volumes, and 33.1 circulations per registered borrower (St. Louis Public Library, unpublished report, 2003). In 2001, the library system served a population of 89,657 children under the age of eighteen, of which 71.5 percent were classified as minority and 65.8 percent as African American (Annie E. Casey Foundation, n. d. a). Also in 2001, 80.4 percent of children were enrolled in a free or reduced lunch program, 57.5 percent received food stamps, 47.2 percent lived in single-parent families, and 36.4 percent were considered to be living in poverty (Annie E. Casey Foundation, n. d. b).

Another challenge St. Louis had been facing was the underachievement of the students in the public school system. During the data collection years, St. Louis city schools were operating with only provisional accreditation status (*Jefferson City News Tribune Online Edition* 2000; St. Louis Public Schools, n. d.). In 2002, only 18.1 percent of seventh graders scored at the "proficient reader" level, and 58.4 percent were not reading at grade level (Missouri Department of Elementary and Secondary Education 2002). In terms of access to computers in the schools, the number of students per Internet-connected computer in 2001 was 12.8, an improvement from the 18.6 figure reported for 2000 (Missouri Department of Elementary and Secondary Education 2002). It was, however, clear that the technology program in the St. Louis library system was crucial for reducing the digital divide in this city. For many youth, the public library was the only place to turn for access to information through technology.

Unexpected Benefits of the CATE OBPE Model

While there were plenty of reasons in terms of potential benefits to local youth for the St. Louis libraries to participate in the research, it also turned out that the library itself experienced unanticipated benefits as a result of immersion in the processes the CATE OBPE model brought. It is probable that many of the same benefits will be seen in other libraries adopting the CATE OBPE model.

One of these benefits was that applying the model improved the relationships between users and staff. Baseline data gathered during the project demonstrated that the city of St. Louis prizes its library and has a strong sense of the value of the library as contributing to the welfare of youth. One of the effects of the planning and evaluation process was that external stakeholders and users experienced firsthand the library staff's responsiveness to the needs of youth, and this increased the positive feelings among both users and staff.

A second unanticipated benefit was that use of the model changed staff members' perceptions of their own work. Understanding what the goals sought in providing technology to youth allowed staff to think about their interactions with users in terms of those goals and provided them with a framework within which to consider how they approached their duties and what they individually could contribute to the desired outcomes.

Another indication of a change in staff orientation toward their own work was apparent in reports from staff of increased cooperation and understanding between departments. Because all departments were oriented to the objectives of the project, the various departments experienced greater insight into their role in helping the library achieve the project goals. This unified purpose allowed the technology, marketing, training, volunteer, adult services, and other departments to include the desired outcomes for youth in thinking and to consider how their work could contribute to these goals.

Another bonus of following the model in St. Louis was that it demonstrated the value of assessment to the library staff. By incorporating data collection methods that were "youth friendly" and providing timely feedback to staff, the relationship between evaluation and the quality of programs and services became a reality that fed the staff's incentive to achieve the desired outcomes in innovative ways. Examples of the program responses developed at the St. Louis Public Library are provided in chapter 9.

Finally, the success of the CATE process suggested that the model is applicable to other services and user groups. Not only was interest in the CATE OBPE model voiced by staff in other departments, links were being made to the viability of using this process in the library's literacy program and outreach to the senior population as well.

In Retrospect

Time has marched on since this project began, and its value becomes clearer with a variety of perspectives. The CATE OBPE model has been introduced, used, and refined in several settings. Its ancillary benefits have been documented. Its concepts have been presented in a wide variety of professional milieus, including an ALSC preconference held in St. Louis in fall 2002, a presentation at the Public Library Association in Seattle in early 2004, and the ALSC's President's Program in summer 2004. In each of these venues, professionals expressed enthusiasm and intense interest in learning the particulars of the CATE OBPE model. On the basis of these user reactions (and others), we have set about to describe in detail in this book how OBPE, especially applied in the CATE OBPE model, can have a positive effect on a library and can, indeed, lead to dynamic youth services. We hope each user sees the sparks of excitement we saw and felt in St. Louis, and we expect that young people will be the ultimate beneficiaries because their library services will be dynamic and better suited to young users' needs.

A Roadmap for Reading

Part I: Introduction to Outcome-Based Planning and Evaluation

Part I provides all necessary background for getting started (part II) and using the CATE OBPE model (part III).

> *Chapter 1: What Is Outcome-Based Planning and Evaluation?* Chapter 1 lays the foundation for the rest of the book. It defines terms and provides a brief history of the planning and evaluation of youth services that leads up to OBPE as it exists in the twenty-first century.

> *Chapter 2: Why Use Outcome-Based Planning and Evaluation in Youth Services?* Chapter 2 points out multiple advantages of the OBPE method for a variety of youth programs.

> *Chapter 3: CATE: An Outcome-Based Planning and Evaluation Model.* Chapter 3 explains the specific model on which many of the recommendations in this book are based. A brief overview, to be detailed later, is given of each phase of the model. One feature emphasized because of its uniqueness is incorporating youth as one of the essential stakeholders at every phase of the planning and evaluation process.

Part II: Getting Started with Outcome-Based Planning and Evaluation

> *Chapter 4: The Leveled Approach to Outcome-Based Planning and Evaluation.* Chapter 4 introduces a means by which OBPE can be applied with three different levels of effort. Also at this stage a decision is made concerning the programs or services to be evaluated.

> *Chapter 5: Developing an Outcome-Based Planning and Evaluation Project.* Chapter 5 becomes relevant after librarians have chosen the programs or services to be developed and their level of effort. Librarians are given hints on preparations necessary for successful OBPE.

Part III: Using the CATE Outcome-Based Planning and Evaluation Model

Chapter 6: Phase 1: Gathering Information: Types. Chapter 6 introduces the first phase of the CATE OBPE model. Emphasis is on gathering existing documents such as the library's strategic plan and policies as well as data from library users, stakeholders, and non-users.

Chapter 7: Phase 1: Gathering Information: Methods. Chapter 7 continues with the first phase of the CATE OBPE model, addressing how to collect the information from users, stakeholders, and non-users and what to do with it once it is collected.

Chapter 8: Phase II: Determining Outcomes. Chapter 8 explains how to combine the results of information gathered in part I with librarians' expertise in determining desired outcomes that will guide the program and service planning in Phase III. It also explains how to create indicators that help tell whether the outcomes (or impacts) have been achieved.

Chapter 9: Phase III: Developing Programs and Services. Chapter 9 shows how the information gathered in Phase I and organized into outcomes in Phase II guides the planning for programs and services.

Chapter 10: Phase IV: Conducting Evaluations. Chapter 10 makes clear the iterative and interactive role of evaluation throughout the planning process as well as the need for a stop-and-look-back approach at logical junctures.

Throughout these chapters, many examples show how to make the CATE OBPE model useful and used—in any library and for projects of any size.

PART I

Introduction to Outcome-Based Planning and Evaluation

One

What Is Outcome-Based Planning and Evaluation?

All doors are hard to unlock until you have the key.

—Robert C. O'Brien,
Mrs. Frisby and the Rats of NIMH

Translated into library lingo, this chapter's epigraph might read, "Knowing whether programs and services produce the results for children and young adults that you and they want or need is hard until you have the right method." Outcome-based planning and evaluation (OBPE) is the key to successful and satisfying library programs and services—successful and satisfying for all involved.

Not everyone agrees on exactly what *outcome* means, but we use it here to mean benefits for or effect on users. This is more than just a result; it denotes a change intended to be positive, following a planned intervention. As used in this book, then, an outcome is the change in attitude, behavior, skill, knowledge, or status that occurs for users after a purposeful action on the part of the library and library staff.

The History of OBPE

The CATE OBPE model incorporates four phases of planning and evaluation: Gathering Information, Determining Outcomes, Developing Programs and Services, and Conducting Evaluations. These phases are thoroughly explained in chapters 3 and 6–10. A look at how planning and evaluation for youth programs and services developed over the past four decades puts the CATE OBPE model into context and highlights the advantages of using it.

Until the 1980s, the development and assessment of library services for youth were considered the professional domain of librarians. Librarians were expected to use their best judgment to determine when new programs and services were needed, to design them, as well as to determine when changes were needed in how things were being done.

To see a contrast to this "librarian knows best" thinking, for a few moments flash forward to October 17, 2002, and a gathering of public librarians at an ALSC Leadership Conference preconference based on the CATE OBPE model. Youth service librarians came to this St. Louis conference from across the United States, representing libraries large and small. Interest in the preconference was intense. Attendance was limited to fifty participants because of auditorium capacity, and long before the registration deadline the meeting was full to capacity, with a lengthy waiting list. As is the custom at a sold-out play or concert, people on the waiting list arrived early and lined up outside the door, hoping for a cancellation.

Participants shared their enthusiasm about OBPE at the end of the day. "I learned a new approach to answering the question of what we can really do to serve the community and the kids." "I now have a skeleton on which to base new programs and changes within the library." "This practical application of outcome-based planning and evaluation makes it doable in our situation." And, demonstrating the change in thinking that comes with OBPE, "I think many librarians tend to do the same programs based on habit. This gives a framework for looking at new possibilities as well as a way to present a very professional 'report' to administration." Not to be overlooked is the practical, "Great tool because most grant writing and project planning is outcome based."

Tracing the development of planning and evaluation of youth services once they were deemed to have some relevance to the practicing children's or young adult librarian sheds light on the OBPE of the early twenty-first century. Today, OBPE consists of methods from the past plus more. OBPE is not, therefore, an entirely new way to plan and evaluate; it is, however, an entirely new way to look at or think about planning and evaluation. OBPE does not require librarians to cast aside practices they have found relevant for assessment of their programs and services; it does, however, extend the usefulness of those practices and place a different emphasis on them in light of new and exciting opportunities. Another way to put this is that practices of the past are necessary but not sufficient to determine the value of programs and services in the lives of youth.

One aspect of the history that unfolds below is that evaluation was and still is sometimes considered a function separate from planning. The model discussed in this book incorporates planning and evaluation as inseparable functions. But more about that later.

How changes in thinking and practice came to be makes an interesting story. Factors outside the library brought the first impetus for change. Fueled by the economic downturn of the 1970s, when costs began to exceed income and competition for funding became a reality for many libraries, interest in evaluating services as a way of securing existing funding or seeking new funding began to grow in many libraries (Lancaster 1977).

Measuring Inputs Came First

At first, evaluation of library services was centered on measuring inputs. This approach implies that quality of program or service is associated with numbers of things a library has to support the programs or services—that is, what is put in, and thus the term *input*. Common means of assessing inputs include measuring library resources such as the number of volumes in the children's or young adult's collections, the size of the children's room or young adult area, and the size of the youth services staff.

For a while, the best thinkers in the profession tried to define the optimal size for a collection, room, or staff. Libraries and many other organizations continue to find it useful to put out "brag sheets" with a variety of input figures, because quantity catches the eye. Some governing boards continue to require these statistics. Many library vendors offer collection analyses that are based on minimum numbers of up-to-date volumes in each Dewey Decimal category or broad subject area, implying that all good libraries should reach this standard.

The problem, of course, is that no matter how many books or computers or chairs there are, they may not be used; no matter how large the physical space is, young users may not come; and no matter how many librarians are there, children may not have their information needs met. Input statistics give us limited information. Often it is necessary to know how many resources the library has, but knowing that is not enough. Quantity of inputs does not tell anything about the difference libraries make in young people's lives. There had to be more to the story.

Measuring Outputs Came Next

Over the course of the 1980s, another means of evaluation was adopted by many libraries. Output measures were recommended by the ALA and were increasingly required by many state libraries for reporting purposes. At first, as was true with each of these modes of evaluation, they were applied just to adult services.

Output measures, instead of looking at a library's resources, focus on how much a service or resource is used. A simple output measure, easy to calculate with automated systems, is circulation of materials. Much library funding is based on this one output measure. If it grows, service is deemed good; if it falls, the library's budget may be in trouble.

One important output measure that is sometimes neglected, because of the difficulty of collecting data, is in-library use. Circulation, as noted, is the principal statistic associated with use of materials. But librarians gradually realized that many youth came into the library, used materials, and left without ever checking anything out. Several methods of documenting in-library use were tried, but none were ideal; it seemed a gigantic and endless job with the cumbersome procedures available at the time.

In the late 1990s, a team of researchers developed a method of measuring in-library use that took advantage of computer technology (Jue, Koontz, and Lance 2001; Koontz, Jue, and Lance 2005). Their approach included tallying in-library use of materials with hand-held devices, commonly known now as personal digital assistants (PDAs). An interesting research finding relevant to Project CATE was that in-library use was higher in lower-income neighborhoods than in high-income neighborhoods. Generally, circulation is higher in upper-income neighborhoods, so including a method that accurately and manageably measures in-library use provides a more balanced picture of who uses library materials. This method was adapted to record observations of youth using computers during the testing of the CATE OBPE model (Gross, Dresang, and Holt 2004; see chapter 6 for more details on this method).

Measures of library output or use by youth might also include how many preschoolers attend a story hour or how many daily hits occur on the teen portion of the library's web page. Perhaps the most common statistic gathered for reference services is a count of the number of reference questions answered by the library staff in a day. Other typical output measures include the number of school classes that come to the library, the annual number of visits the children's librarian makes to public schools, and the number of participants in a summer reading program.

To make these results more meaningful and easier to interpret, circulation and other output measures are calculated per capita in the library's service area. A library with many more children in the service area, for example, may well circulate more children's materials than one with fewer children, but the circulation per capita may be less for the larger service area. This method of dividing numbers of items by the population in the service area makes more accurate comparisons of program and service use possible.

Progress in Evaluation of Programs and Services for Youth

As accountability in public agencies became increasingly prominent in the 1980s, concern grew that children's services in public libraries were lagging behind in efforts to assess programs and services. In 1989, the U.S. Department of Education funded a five-day Leadership Institute on Evaluation Strategies and Techniques for Public Library Services at the University of Wisconsin–Madison. State library consultants, coordinators of children's departments in large metropolitan public libraries and public library systems, and library educators attended.

Analysis of the documentation produced from this conference reveals that there was no holistic model for the planning and evaluation of children's services in use at that time (Robbins et al. 1990). Although presenters acknowledged the need to include children's services in general library planning, this was not reported to be common practice. Evaluation continued to be treated as a more or less isolated function.

Input measures were emphasized in this documentation, but some speakers suggested the use of output measures and the need for measurable objectives for services. There were even speakers who advocated evaluating the impact of services, such as interviews with children about the meaning of what they had read or viewed (Dresang 1990; McDonald and Willett 1990). The conference participants were not accustomed to inquiring about the meaning reading had in the life of their library users—and expressed dismay that anyone would "meddle" with children's privacy by querying them on the meaning of what they chose to read or view. The controversy that ensued turned out to be one of the most memorable events of the conference.

In the 1980s, the ALA published several books that explained how to evaluate public and academic library services using output measures. But it was not until the 1990s that output measures were developed explicitly for children and young adult library services. Virginia Walter (1992, 1995) conducted research and developed output measures for use in the public library for services to children and young adults. Bradburn (1999) also tailored output measures to the school library media center. Output measures were adopted in youth services to varying degrees as dictated by organizational interest and funding requirements.

Rather than replace input measures, output measures added another dimension to library evaluation, allowing a fuller description of library programs and services. It is easy to see that outputs are affected by inputs, and that both remain important evaluation components. In fact, inputs and outputs sometimes become what are explained in chapters 3 and 8 as *indicators* for measuring the impact of a program or service.

Outcomes: What Difference Do Programs and Services Make?

As the push for accountability in government agencies intensified, it became clear that a new approach to evaluation was needed. People became more and more interested in knowing whether expenditures for programs and services, even those that appeared to be well used, made any difference in the lives of those who took advantage of them. Increasingly the "so what" question was posed.

The Government Performance and Results Act (U.S. Congress 1993) made this move for more accountability official. It requires all government agencies to report annually on program results or outcomes. Nongovernmental agencies also recognized the value of this outcome approach. Among nonprofits, the United Way of America and the Kellogg Foundation led the way to outcome-based assessment. The Institute for Museum and Library Services (IMLS), as a government agency, embraced this method of evaluation with a proactive stance. Because of the many public libraries that receive funding from IMLS, either directly or through state agencies, and the accompanying requirement for outcome-based evaluation, by the early twenty-first century *outcome* had become a commonly heard term in public libraries throughout the land.

Interest shifted to the benefits for or effects on users. As had happened with inputs and outputs, the adoption of this new method of evaluation for youth services lagged behind its use for adults. But before long it became apparent once again that the existing measures were still not sufficient to tell the complete story of what the library means to children and young adults. The same questions that had been posed for adult services were heard in relation to children's and young adult services.

In forward-looking public libraries, such as the St. Louis Public Library, knowing that programs and services were popular was not enough. Leading to the CATE project, St. Louis library leaders asked questions about what youth were gaining from their use of technology in the public libraries and how that matched expectations of stakeholders in the community, including the young people themselves. Everyone knew what the program inputs were: including computers donated by the Gates Foundation, more than 600 computers were accessible to children. Everyone knew what the program outputs were. Children signed up for computer use and monthly statistics reflecting use of the computers were gathered. But no one knew what the outcomes were for children or young adults, or even what they ought to be. What difference did it make that young users had technology accessible to them in the public libraries throughout the community? It was impossible to answer this question, even though the computers were in high demand and almost constantly in use.

How Are Outcomes Measured?

One important difference between inputs and outputs, on the one hand, and outcomes, on the other, is that inputs and outputs are most frequently measured quantitatively, whereas outcome measures are sometimes quantitative (words translated into numbers for analysis) but often qualitative (anecdotes or impacts described by the persons involved). With qualitative assessment, a richness and context is added to the data. More about measurement of outcomes appears in chapter 8.

Are All Outcomes Alike?

Asking "What is the impact?" or "What is the outcome?" seems simple enough—until one stops to think about it. One question that has to be addressed is what kind of outcome is of interest. Even that question can be answered in a wide variety of ways (Bertot and McClure 2003; Dresang, Gross, and Holt 2003). Following are some of the many ways people think about an outcome or impact and the desired changes associated with it.

Are the outcomes in the here and now or long-lasting? Libraries invest a considerable amount of resources, financial and human, in summer reading programs. Research has confirmed that children who continue to read during the summer do not lose ground when they return to school in the fall, whereas children who do not read are much more likely to need a great deal of catch-up time when school reopens. Fiore (2005, 11–29) reviews and explicates the reading research relevant to the literacy/learning outcomes of summer reading programs. This research validates the funds that libraries spend to support summer reading, at least in the short-run.

But what are the long-term impacts for children participating in summer reading? Unless those children tested at summer's end are followed in a longitudinal study, the long-term impact of summer reading is not known. Another way of looking at impact is that it occurs in "ripples," with one outcome possibly generating another and then another (Durrance and Fisher 2005, 100).

For example, the sustained reading in the summer program might lead to a child reading most easily and therefore more frequently and with more pleasure in the coming year, which might lead to her personal self-esteem and long-term pleasure in school.

Most librarians start by assessing short-term outcomes, those outcomes or impacts that are apparent throughout the duration of programs or services and at their end if they are not ongoing. Intermittent, "along-the-way" evaluation is called *formative*, and the "at-the-end" evaluation is called *summative*. If the youth involved in the programs are frequent users or if the librarian has continued contact with them through their schools, then assessment of longer-term outcomes for individuals or groups may be accomplished. Often libraries and librarian have long-term outcomes in their plans, since these provide the most return on investment. But short-term outcomes that are apparent in the here and now bring great satisfaction, both to the planners and to those who participate in programs and services.

What types of outcomes are desired? Outcomes sought by libraries or desired by their young users and caretakers are often positive changes in attitude, skills, behavior, knowledge, or status. For example, when the participants at the 2002 preconference on the CATE OBPE model were asked to offer a word or phrase they thought young people in their libraries would apply to technology in the library, many of the words suggested were negative. Some thought kids would say "frustrated," or "waiting," or "crabby staff." When asked to pick the type of outcome or change they would like to see, these librarians said "attitude." The kids were not misbehaving or demonstrating lack of skill or knowledge about the computers in their library, so the librarians were focusing first on a change in attitude. "It is a negative list full of frustrations about technology; we want to make it more positive," said one participant. Those librarians wanted kids to think of the library as a technology-ready and technology-friendly place. To achieve this the librarians would have to determine why the kids' attitudes were poor and what activities or intervention would bring about the desired change. Fortunately, the young computer users in St. Louis did not suffer from negative attitudes. Their desired outcomes fell into the need for skills and knowledge. Each library differs, and each focuses on the outcomes or impacts that stakeholders, including staff and youth, agree are desirable. But thinking this way has a clear impact on planning and evaluation.

Can outcomes apply to places as well as to people? The type of outcomes or impacts the IMLS wants reported are associated with people, the users of programs and services. The focus of the CATE project was on youth ages nine through thirteen who used technology in the St. Louis Public Library. The use of OBPE had impacts on the library as an institution, but these impacts were by-products of the original project. These might be referred to as *institutional outcomes*. But, as Bertot and McClure point out, "there is widespread confusion about what an 'institutional outcome' is" (2003, 605). So outcomes in this book are concerned with people.

How Outcome-Based Evaluation and OBPE Processes Differ

Outcome-based evaluation does not, obviously, "belong" to the field of librarianship. It is, however, considered largely the purview of nonprofit and government agencies, like libraries. Schalock (2001, 6) describes outcome-based evaluation precisely:

> Outcome-based evaluation encompasses the central question of what education, health care, and social service programs set out to achieve for persons receiving them; valued, person-referenced outcomes. It also encompasses what outcome-based evaluation players . . . are requesting of education, healthcare, and social service programs.

In organizations, outcome-based evaluation is almost always considered a component of the planning process, but how integral it is to planning differs from method to method. Even in the first decade of the twenty-first century, most books and articles on outcome-based evaluation discuss it as a somewhat separate component of an overall planning process. Chapters 3–10 demonstrate that, with the CATE OBPE model, planning and evaluation are inseparable, with the planning process incorporating iterative evaluation. This is one of the most important features of the CATE OBPE model. Planning is not finished at any one point in time but rather is ongoing and continually influenced and modified by the frequent evaluation activities. Therefore, the CATE OBPE model is a specific type of outcome-based evaluation.

Also, as explained in chapters 3 and 6, OBPE does not constitute the whole of organizational planning and evaluation but rather must be in accordance with the vision, mission, goals, and objectives of the organization and its strategic plan. It is an excellent means to determine whether a library or a division of the library such as children's or young adult services is meeting organizational goals.

Why Have OBPE for Children and Young Adults?

The CATE OBPE model was developed specifically for youth services. It was designed to answer some of the following questions:

- *Can OBPE be successfully applied to services for children and young adults?* Not everything that works for adult services works for a younger, less stable population. For OBPE, however, the CATE model allows librarians to answer this question with a resounding "yes."

- *Can young people be meaningfully involved throughout the OBPE process?* Involvement of youth in public library program planning has taken hold with the creation of teen advisory boards or councils that assist the library in planning specific activities and events. Teens have also been asked to evaluate the outcomes of programs in which they have been involved. The CATE OBPE model was built in such a way that representative youth could be involved more comprehensively, allowing them to express desired outcomes from the outset and to participate throughout the program by evaluating a library's attainment of those outcomes and by suggesting revisions.

- *Can a model be made interactive to incorporate the fluidity and changing nature of youth, their programs, and their services?* The CATE OBPE model differs from others in its interactive, iterative nature. It is a dynamic model that allows for ongoing evaluation of dynamic programs and services.

The CATE OBPE model, because of its focus on youth and technology, brings to the attention of adults the need to evaluate programs and services for children and young adults. However, although it was designed specifically for planning and evaluation of dynamic youth services, the usefulness of the model is not limited to services and programs for children and young adults, or to computer technology. In fact, at the exit interviews with St. Louis library staff, numerous administrators suggested other ways the model might be used for planning and evaluation. The marketing director had already found a new way of thinking about attracting participants to programs for youth and put it to use. The coordinator of branch services saw great potential in planning services for senior citizens.

What Other Programs for Youth Have Employed OBPE?

When the CATE OBPE model for evaluation was first proposed at the end of 2000, no public library program for youth that had employed an outcome-based evaluation process and reported results publicly could be found, nor did the literature address the impact of technology use by youth in public libraries.

At the time, however, two other projects were initiating or carrying out outcome-based evaluation: Wired for Youth, involving three library systems (Austin, TX; Flint, MI; and Haines, AK), and Public Libraries as Partners in Youth Development, involving nine public library systems (Brooklyn Public Library, NY; Enoch Pratt Free Library, Baltimore, MD; Fort Bend County Libraries, TX; Free Library of Philadelphia, PA; King County Library System, WA; Oakland Public Library, CA; Public Library of Charlotte and Mecklenburg County, NC; Tucson-Pima Public Library, AZ; Washoe County Library System, NV). Since then, both endeavors have made their process and findings available. Neither of these projects, however, emphasized the type of planning and evaluation process the CATE OBPE model incorporates.

The Wired for Youth program used a specific outcome-based evaluation model, How Librarians and Libraries Help. Both the model and the results are reported in Durrance and Fisher (2005). This model was based on inputs, activities, and an assessment of outcomes consistent with the mission of a specific library. In Wired for Youth, outcomes were not defined prior to activities but rather drawn from user accounts. Technological outcomes differed in each community involved, depending on the goals of the program; this happens with any outcome-based evaluation process.

The evaluation of the DeWitt-Wallace/Urban Libraries Council's Public Libraries as Partners in Youth Development Project prepared by the Chapin Hall Center for Children at the University of Chicago (Spielberger et al. 2004) identified outcomes from the four-year project but did not use a specific outcome-based model to guide this evaluation. Evaluators noted that it was not possible to determine the outcomes for the youth exactly; nonetheless, from evidence provided by the youth and by others in the project, the data suggested several valuable outcomes, such as that library-based youth development programs can produce both specific job skills and personal and social development. Another report on this project (Yohalem and Pittman 2003) noted the important lesson that libraries and librarians need to work *with* youth, not simply *for* them. This is also a basic premise of the CATE OBPE model.

Yet another technology-related program using OBPE and focused on youth as part of the planning and evaluation process is the International Children's Digital Library (Druin 2005). Druin, Weeks, and other project leaders from the University of Maryland have involved youth on their design team since the beginning of the project; now they are focusing on twelve young people—from Chicago; Wellington, New Zealand; La Ceiba, Honduras; and Munich, Germany—to help evaluate the impact of using this model. The children will be interviewed once per year for three years to see what difference the books they have read in the digital library program have made in their lives, including their attitudes toward children in other cultures (Druin et al. 2005).

■ ■ ■

Gradually, as the twenty-first century dawned, the planning and evaluation of youth programs and services turned toward outcomes. Librarians for youth now welcome this user-centered approach to programs and services, and OBPE is a key to that approach. OBPE is the right method for knowing whether programs and services produce the desired results for children and young adults. Chapter 2 gives a deeper look into the surprising number of ways OBPE of youth services can positively affect a public library setting.

Why Use Outcome-Based Planning and Evaluation in Youth Services?

Two

What can OBPE do for youth services librarians? There are several different, though compatible, answers to this question. The short answer is that it can help them better serve the children and youth in their community.

Using outcomes provides a systematic way to find out if services are meeting or exceeding the goals set for them, what works best for the people who use the services, and how to change programs and services as the kids in a community change. In addition, outcome-based evaluation helps determine how to best use available resources and get the additional resources needed to provide library service to children in the service area.

In addition to increasing the knowledge of youth services staff, OBPE does the following:

- Helps staff "work smart" by providing a system to measure success and specific information to use to adapt or change programs and services.
- Strengthens library planning and budget allocation.
- Allows a library staff to understand and describe the impact of its program and services on its users by enabling communication among youth services staff and between library departments, including administration, and by enhancing communication with the community, donors, and program partners.
- Provides accountability for public agencies, including libraries. OBPE is required by the federal government and will be increasingly required by

agencies using state and local funds; it is required by some private donors as well.

- Enhances the career paths of individual youth services staff members by adding to their professional skills.

When using outcomes is new to a library, there are some problems to overcome. These include the cost of time and money to use OBPE, the possibility of getting negative results, and the amount of effort to learn the techniques necessary to use OBPE for the first time. But youth services staff will have the opportunity to adopt and adapt OBPE to benefit them in their local situation. The costs of using OBPE are reduced as practices are standardized and more library staff are trained. These costs can also be controlled by choosing the level of effort the library wants to plan for and by starting small as a way of introducing this process to the organization, training staff in its implementation, and allowing all stakeholders to experience the benefits firsthand.

Using Outcomes to "Work Smart"

Though using outcomes takes skill and time, there is a payoff which, in the long run, may save time and extra work. OBPE provides an orderly way to manage programs and services. Once in place it can give instant feedback on a specific program. If children who attend a library program have an easy way to indicate what they liked or did not like about it, what they learned and to what extent outcomes goals were met (changes in skills, attitudes, behavior, etc.), library staff can adapt the next program to meet more closely the needs of kids who attend. If, for example, the purpose of a teen program is to increase knowledge of available age-appropriate websites, program evaluation can be designed to demonstrate the extent to which this outcome is achieved. If the program is not producing the desired results, the youth staff can reevaluate the design of the program to determine how to alter it to achieve the desired results, or to decide if it should even be continued. Evaluation of the program based on input from program participants might prompt the staff to reconsider the types of websites introduced (are they really useful or of interest to teens?), the style of presentation, or other factors. It is easier to get feedback after a program session and make changes than to continue to offer programs that do not meet kids' needs or to wait until low attendance or significant behavioral problems force a rethinking of the program.

OBPE also collects feedback on how youth services as a whole meet the needs of children in the community served. By identifying outcomes or goals in terms of the difference youth services will make to the children served, figuring out how to measure progress toward meeting these goals, and actually measuring or evaluating the benefits gained, staff can set priorities and adapt services to heighten their impact. Perhaps a library wants to know how teen programs affect the kids who attend. Staff can set outcomes after asking questions about individual programs and surveying teens to determine their general impression of the library's offerings and their effects. Finding out if library use makes kids more successful students, gives them confidence, helps them get into college, cheers them up, or entertains them should help library staff know how or if services actually help the teens served. If teens do not know about services offered, improved marketing is suggested. If teens think some services are difficult to use, staff can find ways to reduce barriers to use. Rarely will outcome evaluation be all good news or all bad news, but the opinions and facts collected will help staff target and fine-tune its offerings to increase their impact.

Using Outcomes to Strengthen Planning and Budgeting

Part of the responsibility of youth services staff is to use the resources available to give the most service to the most people. Typically, resources include budget, staff skills and knowledge, staff time, collection, and partnerships. The goal is to coordinate and prioritize use of these resources over time. Youth services staff often participate in the library's planning and budgeting and, in turn, set goals and allocate resources for youth services activities. Using outcomes during planning ensures that user needs are identified and community goals set. It also provides another way to measure systematically the community benefits of using library services, one that augments the more traditional measures of expenditures and library usage. Adding outcomes to the planning process focuses on the results of library service for library users.

For youth services it may be particularly important to use outcomes to identify needs, since children do not typically have a voice in planning or decision making. Children do not vote, do not normally serve on library boards or in city government, do not pay taxes or fund library activities. OBPE can provide direct input to goal setting from the recipients of youth services, including children, parents, teachers, caregivers, and other stakeholders. The specific information gathered from youth changes the focus of what is generally good for children to what a specific library can do during a specific year to meet the needs of the actual children who will use the library.

A traditional approach to planning includes inputs—the available budget and resources—and outputs—what the library did and how many people used it. A library spends collection development money and uses staff expertise to build a collection to serve children (inputs). At the end of the year, the library measures the usage of the children's collection by reporting circulation and in-house use of materials (outputs). If circulation is high or increases, the collection effort is a success; if circulation decreases, explanations are sought.

If OBPE is added to this process, children and families have an opportunity to identify the impacts they desire from children's use of the collection. Library staff can then set user outcome goals such as "Primary-age children will become regular readers by using the library's collection." Indicators of success might include how often children and parents read the books they check out, and if they come to the library often. Information about difficulties families have finding books of interest or using the library also helps youth services staff find ways to reach outcome goals. Users might report that they do not find enough easy reading books to choose from in general, or books that interest an individual child; they might report that loan periods are not long enough.

With outcome information, collection development decisions can be made on the basis of user success as well as library use. The library can justify buying books for new readers if users confirm that using library books increases reading behavior of the children in the community. Planners can increase the numbers of easy-reading books or maintain the current collection level, depending on the results of OBPE.

Using Outcomes to Communicate about Youth Services

Just as using outcomes helps youth services staff make good decisions and set goals, it can help library staff communicate both within the library and externally with taxpayers, elected officials, partners, or the community at large. The United Way of America (2003) reports that the two most identified advantages of outcome-based evaluation are that it focuses staff on shared goals and helps to communicate results or achievements to stakeholders. In fact, 88 percent of four hundred United Way agency directors reported experiencing these communication-related benefits after using outcome-based evaluation. These directors also found that using outcomes helped them compete for resources. Learning from the experience of these service agencies, youth services library staff can gain focus as a staff, communicate to other library staff not providing services to youth, and obtain funding both during the library's budget process and from external granting agencies.

Because outcomes are stated in specific terms and measures of progress toward success are described explicitly as a part of setting outcome goals, it is easier for staff to understand what should be accomplished by day-to-day activities. While various staff members may be responsible for specific aspects of the youth program (preschool storytimes or homework help may be provided by different people), each service can be designed to meet outcomes identified during the planning process. In one-person youth services departments, outcomes keep the work and evaluation of services to different target audiences done by this person more focused and coordinated. For example, if the library has outcomes related to supporting pre-reading skill development, reading, and literacy, the programs for each age group can be tied to reading themes and age-appropriate reading activities.

Since youth services exist within the library, it is important the non–youth services staff understand (and support) the department's work. Outcomes can help other library staff understand what can be accomplished by youth services and how they fit into the larger work of the library. If the library sets a goal to improve the literacy of the community, understanding the importance of and the ability of youth services to strengthen reading behaviors of young people will help engender cooperation and support of all library staff for library reading programs for children.

Another way outcomes help youth services staff communicate is with people and agencies outside the library. Since outcome goals involve people in the community and are stated in terms of changes or growth of community members, it is easier for the community to understand and value activities associated with these goals. Because outcomes focus not on changes at the library but on how (in the case of youth services) children learn, grow, and change, they are effective in "telling the library's story" to the public and to public officials.

Here's an example. A library may have always reported the number of children who attended story programs as part of an annual report. Although it would be unusual for the library's board, members of the public, or city officials to oppose story programs, the value of such programs may not be clear to those outside the library. If the library staff sets outcomes based on the opinions of community stakeholders for story programs and measures the changes in skill, knowledge, behavior, or attitudes of those attending, then the connection of story programs to successful reading of the community's children will be clear and the answer to "why is this important?" easily answered.

At the St. Louis Public Library, staff developed project outcomes on the basis of input from a variety of stakeholders, and programs were developed to respond to these outcomes. The outcomes included a list of skills and attitudes of young children that could be improved by participation in family literacy programs, including story programs. The participants were families in which adults read at or below the fifth-grade level.

Two major outcome goals set after focus groups with parents and care-givers were that children would spend more time reading or listening to stories at home and school (change of behavior) and that children would have a positive attitude toward reading. Outside evaluators found that parents, day-care workers, and teachers reported that children spent more time each week reading, asked to read more often, and talked about the books they read more often (Lévesque 1999). Because the library could report how many children and families participated in the program *and* how the program helped children be readers, school administrators acknowledged that the program helped the school meet its goal of all children reading by the third grade. Because outcome-based evaluation showed results for children and teachers, the school understood much more clearly the reason cooperation between public library and school benefited children and helped the school meet its goals. The school staff did not see public library programs as "extra" but as directly related to educational goals. As a result, public library programs were reported to the state school accrediting agency as evidence that the school was making progress toward state standards, and the school now facilitates scheduling of public library programs and distributes information about public library programs and services.

Outcomes Provide Accountability

OBPE is becoming the norm for libraries and other service agencies. After the U.S. Congress passed the Government Performance and Results Act in 1993, every federal government agency was required to establish measurable goals. IMLS began to use outcome-based evaluation to comply with this law. IMLS is a federal agency that fosters leadership and innovation in the nation's libraries. It requires state libraries to use outcomes and requires that libraries receiving IMLS or state Library Services and Technology Act (LSTA) grants include outcome evaluation in all funded projects. Some state and local governments have adopted outcome standards, so libraries may be able to adapt local outcome procedures if they are part of a city government that has used outcome evaluation. Virginia Walter mentions the need to develop outcomes evaluation for youth services in her *Children & Libraries: Getting It Right* (2001), and in 2004 the ALSC offered a full day of training on outcome-based evaluation of youth services at its national institute in Minneapolis. The ALA has published *How Libraries and Librarians Help: A Guide to Identifying User-Centered*

Outcomes (Durrance and Fisher 2005) and will publish a book on outcomes as part of the Public Library Association's Planning for Results series.

Many government and nonprofit agencies have been using outcome-based evaluation since the mid-1990s. In 2003, United Way of America surveyed service organizations from around the country about each organization's use of outcome measures. It found that more than 20,000 agencies and programs were shifting to the use outcome evaluation and were using evaluation findings to increase the effectiveness of services offered (United Way of America 2003, v). It is likely that agencies receiving United Way funding locally are beginning to use outcome evaluation to assess the services they provide, including traditional youth-serving agencies such as the Girl Scouts and Boy Scouts as well as umbrella agencies with youth programs such as Catholic Charities and the YMCA.

Because so many government and youth-serving agencies are using some form of outcome measurement, youth services staff may find using outcome evaluation increasingly necessary to receive funds or to partner with other community agencies.

Using Outcomes Is a Professional Asset

As outcome evaluation becomes required and more widely used, library staff members who can successfully apply it will be sought and put in positions of leadership. Youth services staff who plan a career in public library service will find that obtaining these skills is an asset. Libraries will need employees, whether at the MLS level or as pre-professionals, who can participate in outcomes planning. Getting the training and having the experience of using outcomes will provide opportunities to grow and advance professionally.

Such skills as writing surveys and collecting and analyzing the data from them, effectively interviewing children and adults, and conducting successful focus groups are useful in building a career. Staff members who can ask the right questions and understand the answers from the various target groups will be able to provide leadership in library planning. For youth services workers who wish to consult or work on grant projects in public libraries, outcome-based evaluation skills will be required; consultants with these skills will attract clients.

IMLS offers training in outcome-based evaluation for librarians, and library schools are beginning to offer courses to help train professionals in the technique. For example, the College of Information at Florida State University offered a credit course on outcome-based evaluation (funded in part by IMLS) to master's students in 2003. The course was well received. Many state libraries offer training and are developing standards of outcome use as part of library grants and continuing education activities. As training becomes available, OBPE skills will be expected for youth services staff responsible for evaluating services and programs.

Overcoming Resistance to Using Outcomes

Like all forms of evaluation, outcomes are best used when they are accepted by all levels of staff, including direct service providers, managers, library administration, and library board members. For various reasons, one or more of these groups may not be comfortable using outcomes. OBPE may be viewed as costly and time consuming, as difficult to do successfully, as generating more work (and more paperwork!), or there may be concern about what to do with the results of outcome evaluation. Some staff may be uncomfortable using direct input from the public, particularly from children, in library decision making. Some staff just do not like change. It is wise to understand the library environment and work to address staff concerns as OBPE is begun.

Controlling Outcome Costs

IMLS suggests that a library should budget 7–10 percent of a program's budget to cover the cost of OBPE (IMLS 2002, 7). Actual costs depend on the level of the evaluation and the staff's experience with the techniques used. Costs may include those for hiring outside evaluators to collect and analyze data, printing surveys, or mailing questionnaires. Staff time is a likely expense and may include the cost of training. It is certainly possible to use grant funds such as LSTA to cover some of the costs of outcome evaluation, but not all programs and services are supported by grants, and regardless of who is paying for the evaluation, libraries will want to control the costs of outcome evaluation. In any case, outcome evaluation must have a budget to ensure that there are no surprises in controlling its costs.

Another cost consideration is that of time and resources wasted by not using outcome evaluation in planning youth programs and services. Planning, producing, and advertising programs for children that are not of interest to children, or that do not meet their needs, are expensive and wasteful. If even 10 percent of the library's children's programs miss the mark of helping children or attracting an audience, the cost of outcome evaluation could be made up by designing and presenting more effective programs.

Controlling Time Needed for Outcome Evaluation

Staff can resent the time spent on OBPE if they see it as taking them away from direct service or believe that it is too difficult. Again, it is possible to overcome these objections by acknowledging that evaluation takes time and making clear what skills are needed to use it. Youth services managers should understand that some staff members must be trained to collect data or conduct evaluations. Only a few staff will need to design data collection or analyze results. Well-planned evaluation of any kind uses the least amount of effort to meet the requirements for nonbiased results. Time for evaluation can also be minimized by starting with simple techniques, sampling, and piloting new activities to eliminate problems before much of the staff is involved. Staff should have the goal to keep outcome evaluation as simple as possible and to make sure all involved know their role and have the skills and knowledge to do their part. And the evaluator needs to present outcome evaluation as a healthy part of providing service.

Controlling Paperwork

Libraries have a strong tradition of measurement and evaluation, and much of it generates extra paperwork. Evaluation does call on librarians' considerable records management skills, and outcome evaluation is no exception. For example, data collection instruments such as surveys and focus group questions must be created, the data collected and analyzed, and reports written to discuss findings and their implications for further program and service development. All of this generates paperwork. In many cases, libraries are already engaged in counting the number of programs provided, the number of attendees, and other kinds of output data. There is already a lot of paper moving and number tabulating, and no one wants to add more. On the other hand, librarians have been keeping track of things professionally forever, so they are "in training" for the further paper/records management needed for success with OBPE.

Librarians can take advantage of electronic management, which simplifies and to some extent controls the extra clerical work generated by outcome evaluation. At the St. Louis Public Library, for example, staff called up a questionnaire checklist on PDAs, asked children questions, and noted the answers by electronic check-off. Data were stored electronically and sent to the evaluator by e-mail, then reports were generated online. It took staff about ten minutes to learn to use the PDA and record data correctly. At focus groups, observers took notes on laptops, and a digital camera documented program activities. Recording activities in electronic format minimized the effort to use and report data.

Although a paper-based questionnaire may be the best or only way to collect information from some users, electronic records management helps reduce the effort to collect and keep track of data. It is also possible that a professional group or IMLS may provide data management tools in the future that will help libraries manage data more easily. The Girl Scouts, for example, publish an outcome evaluation manual for junior Scout leaders that includes a tool recorded on CD to help data collection and management (Hwalek, Essenmacher, and Juntunen 2002). Records management will get easier and more likely be in electronic form in the future. Although outcome evaluation requires additional clerical work, it can be controlled and integrated into procedures librarians have already used to minimize the clerical tasks.

Dealing with Negative Results

Some staff worry that the purpose of OBPE is to show weaknesses in a library's services or to show staff mistakes. It may give library users a chance to complain about the library or ask for new services the library cannot provide. Some staff think listening to library patrons raises patron expectations that the library will be able to respond positively to all suggestions. Some staff may have specific concerns about involving young people in evaluation or using the results of that evaluation in library planning.

One way to make staff more comfortable with such concerns is to run practice sessions with patrons or use case studies as examples of how OBPE works and in particular how libraries deal with negative results. This should include how the library will respond to the people who participate in focus groups, surveys, or interviews. For example, in one of the St. Louis Public Library's first focus groups with young people, there was a truly overwhelming positive tone. This in itself made staff more comfortable about asking patrons directly what they thought of library services. In addition, the kids in the focus groups identified problems staff agreed with, so they realized that these young people were "on their side" and would help call attention to problems and identify ways of solving them.

Of course, these focus groups also identified complaints, and there were negative comments about specific staff members and services. The biggest complaint about staff was occasional grumpiness, but this was balanced by comments that staffers were fair (a strong value for pre-teens), smart, and helpful. The reported "grumpy" staff members were a bit defensive but could identify ways they could be more welcoming; the staff eventually developed a formal welcoming procedure. Kids wanted more computers (so did staff) and better access to them, and they thought one particular branch should be painted some color other than gray. During branch renovation, a computer room with three times as many computers was created, and the branch was redone in rich Victorian yellows and pinks (the branch had first opened in 1906). Youth access was improved by designating some computers as "kids-first" machines during nonschool hours, so young people did not have to ask adult patrons to let them use their scheduled time. The staff felt comfortable with these changes and encouraged the administration to hold focus groups about each branch.

Sometimes kids (and adults) suggest things that cannot be done or are based on inaccurate information. In St. Louis, kids complained about overdue fines and rules in general. The fine structure was not changed. Many of the complaints about rules had been caused by poor library explanations of those rules. Listening to young people talk did help staff do a better job explaining rules and collecting fines. Kids seemed satisfied that library staffers listened and were respectful of their opinions.

Some patron suggestions may not seem realistic in the short term but can still result in changes over time. One complaint from a St. Louis focus group was that the library staff was too old. This was not exactly a morale builder for staff members, and at first there did not seem to be any way to address this concern. In fact, with luck, it would only get worse; over time, staff would just get older. During the next several years, though, the library was able to use grant money to start a teen volunteer program that brought high school students into the library to work with younger children and another program to hire college students to work in the library after school. Both programs provided young people to work with pre-teens and children. Kids reported that they felt more welcome and that the staff seemed friendlier.

OBPE supplies data and suggests directions on the basis of user comments, but it is up to staff to chart the library's response to user data. Patrons often identify the same problems as staff, and dealing with negative feedback can often result in positive changes for staff. Experience with OBPE and understanding how negative comments are likely to be handled will help staff feel more comfortable about seeking user input.

■ ■ ■

Libraries that have used OBPE find that it has helped adjust services to the actual needs of those served. Patron input can help youth services staff make good use of their resources and show the results of specific programs and services. Using outcomes helps youth services compete for resources within the library and helps the library compete for resources from city government, taxpayers, and outsider funders. Using OBPE helps communicate the value of good youth services by documenting the impact of that work on the lives of users. It clarifies which problems users would like solved. If the reason libraries offer special services to youth is to help young people be successful, then outcomes need to be used to help maximize that impact. The true measure of success for youth service advocates and service providers is the benefit children, their families, and their teachers receive from library services. OBPE is an essential technique for measuring, refining, and maximizing benefits to young users.

Three

CATE

An Outcome-Based Planning and Evaluation Model

Project CATE came on the scene at the beginning of a new transition in program and service evaluation. Although input and output measures continue to provide useful information for assessing library programs and services, they fall short in terms of providing information about the impact of the library on the lives of users. Recognition of this gap in the information provided by typical project assessments led increasingly to the adoption of outcome-based evaluation, which is focused on understanding how the work libraries do actually helps people (Rudd, n. d.).

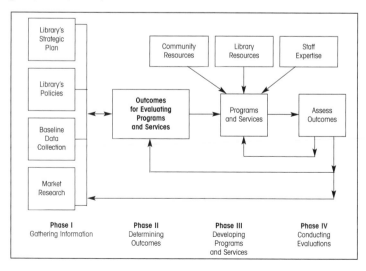

| Phase I | Phase II | Phase III | Phase IV |
| Gathering Information | Determining Outcomes | Developing Programs and Services | Conducting Evaluations |

The CATE OBPE model combines outcome-based evaluation methods with planning processes many libraries are familiar with, such as community analysis, user needs assessment, strategic planning, and the fundamentals of evaluation. This means that libraries already engaged in strategic planning will find the CATE OBPE model easy to integrate into established procedures. This also means that the model will provide libraries that have not already done so a starting point for the planning and evaluation process.

Components of the CATE OBPE Model

The CATE OBPE model describes a continuous process of planning and evaluation that progresses over four phases of activity. Each phase of the process is dependent on the phases before it and feeds the phases that follow it. In the model's flowchart, the four phases are labeled along the bottom, and arrows demonstrate the relationships between phases. It is important to note the iterative nature of planning, development, and evaluation described in the model. The CATE OBPE model is directed toward the delivery of outcomes and recognizes that desired outcomes change over time and therefore must be reassessed periodically. The result is a process that keeps staff actively engaged in understanding the impact and effectiveness of their work, ensuring that it is responsive to user needs.

The four phases of the CATE OBPE model are as follows:

Phase I: Gathering Information

Phase II: Determining Outcomes

Phase III: Developing Programs and Services

Phase IV: Conducting Evaluations

These phases describe how to plan, design, implement, and evaluate programs and services that are focused on attaining specific outcome goals. What follows here is a general overview of each phase. Detailed discussions of how to complete these phases are provided in parts III and IV of this book.

Phase I: Gathering Information

The first step in using the CATE OBPE model is to develop a clear understanding of where programs and services fit within the context of the library and the community it serves. The inputs to this process are the library's strategic plan and policies and may include information gathered about the library or the community. Phase I also introduces the use of market research techniques to support the development of programs and services that target desired outcomes.

THE LIBRARY'S STRATEGIC PLAN

Understanding the library's strategic plan is fundamental to defining the scope of the kinds of programs and services that will best support the library's general plan for meeting the information needs of its community. Several kinds of documentation produced as part of strategic planning can provide important input concerning the library's mission and user information needs. However, in libraries where planning has not been formalized or has not been performed for five years or more, it may not be possible to rely on such documentation. In such cases, it is necessary to gather missing or out-of-date information. Strategic planning is discussed in detail in chapter 6.

Strategic planning documentation that is important in Phase I includes the library's

- vision and mission statements
- choice of service roles
- data collected and reports written as part of a community and user information needs analysis
- planning documents that discuss the strengths, weaknesses, opportunities, and threats (SWOTs) identified for the library
- goals and objectives derived from the strategic planning process

THE LIBRARY'S POLICIES

A review of library policies is important for understanding the context within which programs and services can be designed, developed, and delivered. Many factors shape the development of library policy, which in turn affect program and service activities in the library. For instance, library policy can be influenced by government legislation, professional standards as explicated by the ALA, as well as local community standards.

The library policy that is likely to be most relevant to the development of programs and services for youth is the policy concerning intellectual freedom. Often this policy is expressed in collection development documents or in acceptable use statements developed specifically to address issues of Internet access.

Library policies concerning access to technology by youth, including acceptable use policy, increasingly come into play in plans for program and service development. These policies may include rules that help manage technology use in the library and through remote access and address such questions as these: Does the library provide separate computers for youth? Is parental consent required for youth to use technology in the library? Is a library card required to use technology? Are there limits on the amount of time individuals can use the computer (at one sitting, or per week, month, etc.)? Are limits placed on how many people can be at a computer at the same time?

BASELINE DATA COLLECTION

To understand the impact of current programs and services fully, it is important to have a baseline understanding of what current use looks like as a first step toward thinking about evaluation. Knowing what current use looks like provides a benchmark for comparing current performance to professional standards or to the performance of other similar libraries. Baseline data are also important for planning future assessments of performance, since they provide a point of comparison for demonstrating the improvements expected from new programs and services.

Baseline data can come from several different sources and can be used for a variety of purposes, and Project CATE illustrates many of these. To develop outcomes with the CATE OBPE model, a variety of baseline data were needed. To fully understand issues of access for youth, it was necessary to

- identify aspects of computer use (or non-use) that might represent important factors for thinking about the kinds of technological programs and services needed
- identify which, if any, subgroups among youth to target
- obtain an objective view of user skill levels, usage patterns, and interests concerning use of technology
- determine the appropriate level of programs and service
- inform the collection and management of electronic resources for youth

Another reason to collect baseline data is to allow for the development of goals and objectives related to programs and services. Understanding the current state of technology use in Project CATE provided a starting point for thinking about how much change was needed and how quickly desired changes could be made. Baseline data also represented a point of comparison for measuring the impact of new programs and services. Without an understanding of how youth used technology at the library, it would not have been possible in

Project CATE to measure the full impact of technological programs and services or the effect of the CATE OBPE model.

Baseline data from stakeholders is also important and was used in Project CATE to elicit a variety of perspectives. First and foremost, youth themselves were asked what outcomes they hoped for as a result of their use of technology in the public library. They were asked not only about what they knew and did but also about what they did not know and wanted to learn. They were asked what worked in the library's current approach and what was needed to improve technological services. They were asked why they came to the library to use technology and to what extent they thought it important for the library to provide them technological services.

In addition to the voices of youth, the perceptions of adults interested in youth were sought. Parents, teachers, community leaders, school library media specialists, public librarians, and other library staff gave their views about the desired goals for use of technology by youth.

Baseline data can be collected by a variety of methods. In Project CATE, the methods included surveys, focus groups, and in-library observations. These methods are explained in more depth in chapter 7.

MARKET RESEARCH

The data gathering techniques used in market research are the same ones commonly used in community and user needs assessments, such as surveys and focus groups. The difference is that in a marketing approach the emphasis is on developing programs and services targeted to a specific audience in partnership with that audience.

In the case of Project CATE, the audience for the development of technological programs and services for youth included both youth and adults interested in their welfare. Two valuable approaches to program development were combined: the involvement of children in product development and marketing strategies (Druin 2005; McNeal 1999) and the collection of adult views of children's needs, an approach that has long been standard practice. When the participation of both youth and adults interested in their welfare is elicited, a complete assessment of the viability and benefits of planned programs and services can be achieved.

Phase II: Determining Outcomes

In Phase II, the information gathered in Phase I is examined and used to identify the outcomes that become the focus of program and service development for the current planning cycle and the criteria to be used to assess success of the programs and services. Project CATE adopted the outcome categories described by the United Way of America (1996), in which outcome measures are expected to describe how projects have made a difference in the lives of the people they are targeted to help in terms of effecting changes in their skill, knowledge, behavior, attitude, or status.

The double-headed arrow that connects Phase I and Phase II in the model's flowchart demonstrates the dependence between these two sets of activities. The decisions made in Phase II follow from the information gathered in Phase I, which provides a snapshot of what the community, the library, and youth in the community look like and want at one point in time. To remain responsive to stakeholders, it is important to revisit and reassess the information gathered in Phase I periodically for any changes in the community or library that will affect the choice of desired outcomes or the way they are measured.

The determination of desired outcomes and how to measure them is informed by the library's place in the community, the resources committed to programs and services for youth, and input received from youth and other stakeholders, as described above. The choice of one or multiple outcomes to pursue is determined by what the community wants youth to achieve or experience as well as by the functions the library serves in the community. The process of determining desired outcomes and developing criteria for evaluation is described in detail in chapter 8.

Phase III: Developing Programs and Services

The goal of Phase III is to determine what the library will do to achieve the desired outcomes selected in Phase II. This sequence ensures that the programs and services purchased, designed, or developed by the library are oriented from the beginning toward the goal of achieving the desired outcomes for youth who utilize the library. The outcomes determined in Phase II provide a framework for the development of programs and services but, as the CATE OBPE model shows, additional inputs and considerations must be taken into account in this phase.

The library exists within the context of its community. Before moving ahead, it is important to consider what similar or complementary resources are available in the community, as well as the library's own resources and staff expertise. It may not be reasonable to duplicate services that are available elsewhere in the community, and it may be possible through community partnerships to provide expanded services to youth in the community. The assessment of staff expertise also reveals what kinds of development are possible or require staff training before they can be implemented.

Phase III is an important hub of activity in the CATE OBPE model. In addition to its close connection to the determination of desired outcomes, this phase also begins the active application of evaluation activities designed to assess how programs and services are achieving their goals. The design and development of programs and services include plans for evaluation, and it is expected that programs and services will be assessed as they are implemented and adjusted as necessary to ensure relevance and the realization of outcome goals. Programs and services that are not providing the desired outcomes and cannot be improved are dropped.

The outcomes determined in Phase II can also be used to guide the adoption of commercial products and services, for these too can be assessed for their contributions to desired outcomes. The procedures for assessing available resources and expertise and developing outcome-based programs and services, along with example program responses from Project CATE, are described in chapter 9.

Phase IV: Conducting Evaluations

As discussed above, CATE OBPE evaluation is a continuous process that is integrated into the design and delivery of programs and services. This means that the desired outcomes and methods used to measure them as identified in Phase II continue to be relevant. It is important that any changes to the outcome goals feed into the development, delivery, and assessment of programs and services. Likewise, a periodic summary evaluation, one that takes a holistic approach to assessing work with youth in the library, is needed to determine if services are achieving the desired outcome-based goals and, if not, why. It may be that programs and services need to be improved or discontinued. It is also possible that the library and community have changed since the previous planning cycle, and evaluation may point to the need to gather more information to ensure that programs and services remain responsive to user and community needs.

All of these processes are denoted by the arrows leading from Phase IV back to each of the other phases. It is at this point in the process that the dynamic and iterative features of the CATE OBPE model are fully demonstrated. Planning, design and development, and evaluation are integrated into a system that is self-updating, ensuring both responsiveness to the changing environment and the successful delivery of high-impact programs and services for youth. The specifics of conducting evaluations as a continuous process are described in chapter 10.

Assumptions behind the CATE OBPE Model

All problem-solving approaches are based on assumptions that may or may not be explicit. Several assumptions are important to successful use of the CATE OBPE model. The adoption or adaptation of the model is most comfortable and useful in environments that share these assumptions:

- Evaluation is continuous.
- Children are competent and seek connection with the digital world.
- Children have a right to access information.
- Input from children, adults, and organizations interested in children is needed to both develop and evaluate programs and services.
- Desired outcomes for children's library use can be identified by market research.
- Strategic planning, market research, and outcome-based evaluation are useful tools for program and service development and assessment.
- The library staff and community stakeholders are fully committed to the process.
- The library can perform adequate data collection and synthesize findings into statements of desired outcomes.

Why Use the CATE OBPE Approach to Evaluate Programs and Services?

The CATE OBPE model is a comprehensive planning and evaluation tool that integrates strategic planning with outcome-based evaluation and market research techniques. This means that it can be easily integrated into existing planning processes or used to provide a framework for developing a planning process that is responsive to community needs. It also provides an opportunity to integrate planning for youth services into the larger issues of the organization as a whole, strengthening the library's overall effort to be responsive to the community. Additionally, because the CATE OBPE model uses outcome-based evaluation techniques, it meets the evaluation criteria increasingly required by government, foundations, and other funding sources.

The CATE OBPE model offers a leveled approach. CATE OBPE is a flexible model that can be implemented at different levels of effort. The leveled approach, discussed in chapter 4, allows libraries to apply the model at the level of effort that suits internal considerations such as staff expertise, experience with evaluation processes, resource availability, and administrative support.

The model can be used to plan, develop, and assess a single program or service, a group of programs on a common topic or theme, or the full range of services provided by youth (or other departmental) services.

The CATE OBPE model involves all stakeholders. CATE OBPE fills a gap in the evaluation literature by providing a comprehensive model that brings new methods to the evaluation of youth services. These new methods include outcome-based evaluation, which in turn focuses on the impact of programs and services on the lives of users, and market research, which allows for the development of programs and services in partnership with users. These methods ensure that all stakeholders, youth as well as adults and agencies interested in youth, have a voice in the determination of desired outcomes and the development of programs and services designed to achieve those outcomes.

The CATE OBPE model provides a process that clarifies the aims of programs and services for all stakeholders and helps cultivate a culture of evaluation and learning in the professional activities of the library. Because programs and services are developed with specific outcomes in mind, personnel understand the objectives behind the performance of tasks and are better able to assess performance and make suggestions for improvement.

The CATE OBPE model allows sharing and comparison among participating libraries. By providing a formal, holistic model for planning and evaluation, CATE OBPE offers a standard approach that allows comparison and sharing of program and service developments among libraries that have demonstrated vitality for the attainment of specific outcomes. The experience of participating libraries can then be reviewed for similarities in size and community structure to improve understanding of what type of programming has been successful in attaining specific outcomes for youth.

■   ■   ■

Outcome-based evaluation is becoming the norm for many libraries as well as other types of service agencies. Increasingly, funding agencies such as the IMLS, state libraries and agencies that administer LSTA grants, and foundations such as the United Way and the W. K. Kellogg require outcome-based evaluation in all funded projects. But the benefits of using a planning and evaluation process such as that offered by CATE OBPE are greater than the short-term benefit of responding to these requirements. Understanding the impact of programs and services in terms of their effect on users' lives can resonate in many directions. The following chapters provide a roadmap for using OBPE to determine and achieve the outcomes that make sense for the library and its community and for sharing these accomplishments with others.

PART II

Getting Started with Outcome-Based Planning and Evaluation

The Leveled Approach to Outcome-Based Planning and Evaluation

Four

> "I never knew words could be so confusing," Milo said. . . .
> "Only when you use a lot to say a little," answered Tock.
>
> —Norton Juster, *The Phantom Tollbooth*

What do Milo and Tock have to do with the OBPE process for youth services in libraries? The answer becomes clear with the substitution of a few phrases:

"I never knew outcome-based planning and evaluation could be so confusing," Librarian A said. . . .

"Only when you use a lot to do a little," answered Librarian B.

Librarians may sometimes feel overwhelmed as they approach an OBPE process; for this reason, it is an important part of the planning process to focus on exactly what the scope of the planning and evaluation effort will be and why. Also, each member of the library staff must know at what level his or her involvement is expected or needed. Limiting the project to the specific information desired, no more and no less, reduces anxiety and makes good sense.

The purpose of this chapter, then, is to make clear that OBPE activities may vary in intensity, duration, and focus. They may involve only one or two staff members and a handful of users, or they may involve much of the staff and numerous users. Some evaluations take place in the context of baseline data previously collected for much larger projects. Often it is not necessary to conduct a huge community analysis because this has recently been done.

Choosing an Appropriate Level of Effort

The leveled approach is based on a precise understanding of the nature or complexity of the program or service to which OBPE is applied and then an appropriate choice of level of effort to accomplish the desired outcomes. Perhaps one useful way to think about the process is to remember the information behavior theory known as the principle of least effort. It has been demonstrated by substantial research over several decades that people often "minimize the effort required to obtain information" (Case 2005, 291). Although this is not always optimal behavior in the short term, it is wise to recognize it as a normal and sometimes desirable approach to get things done. With the hurried life all librarians experience, it is important to expend just the right amount of effort.

In addition to the character of the program or service involved, other factors make the OBPE process more or less intense. Appropriate responses to factors like the following in each OBPE level can both simplify and enhance the process:

- Persons responsible for the project
- Extent and expected longevity of the project
- Groups of stakeholders included
- Numbers of stakeholders included in each group
- Types of information gathered
- Methods by which the information is gathered
- Numbers of questions asked to obtain the information needed
- Methods of analyzing the collected data
- Ways of using the collected data

The more straightforward and uncomplicated the descriptions of these factors, the simpler the OBPE process will be. If the extent and expected longevity of the project is "one program offered on four occasions," then the OBPE will be Level I (explained below), the quickest type of OBPE. The more complex the descriptions of these factors, the more likely the entire OBPE process will be multifaceted. Multifaceted OBPE is referred to as Level III. For example, if those responsible for the project are "the library director and the board of trustees," then an extensive OBPE process is most likely. The same principle applies to all aspects of a program or service.

In chapters 5 and 9 the factors to be considered in OBPE are discussed more thoroughly. Chapters 6–8 give a fairly comprehensive view of all the types of data that can be collected, analyzed, and used in an OBPE process. These chapters do not suggest, however, that all means of data collection should be used in every project; rather, these are the methodologies from which one can choose, using care to choose only those directly relevant to the audience and desired outcomes.

The leveled approach to OBPE provides the librarian and library staff with a powerful planning tool. Upfront, a decision is made about the level of effort to be applied to the project at hand. The leveled approach gives a librarian the proper mindset to pick and choose more or less depending on the focus of the OBPE.

Librarians who set out to implement the CATE OBPE model must first decide which of the three levels fits their current situation and planning and evaluation needs: Level I, a single program, offered once or repeated; Level II, a group of programs on a common topic or theme; or Level III, a multifaceted program.

These planning and evaluation levels are separate but related entities. They can be used independently, or they can be nested and carried out simultaneously, as shown here. Together they strengthen the evaluation process. Starting from the center, simple and quick OBPE undertaken at Level I can stand alone and is probably the most common type of OBPE in which individual youth librarians are involved. Although each level may be implemented independently of the others, planning and evaluation at Level II are informed and enhanced by data collected by Level I activities. A similar statement can be made for a Level III OBPE exercise: it can be informed and enhanced by Level I and Level II data assessments, and it definitely contributes to Level II and Level I planning and evaluation.

When choosing Level I, librarians must be aware of the implications for larger programs or efforts of which the single program may be a part. Likewise, those employing OBPE at Level II must recognize how the results of this program evaluation relate to a larger organizational effort or to a single program. This admonition brings to mind the oft-cited meditation of John Donne, "No man is an island, entire of itself," but in this case it becomes "No OBPE is an island, entire of itself."

Neither the outcomes nor the possible effects on planning are intended to be comprehensive. Notice as you read the following examples how the desired outcome helps focus the planning process. How such outcomes are developed or measured are further described in chapters 6–8. The examples in this chapter are figuratively to get your feet wet. The comments following each example give some context and suggest how the CATE OBPE process makes it more likely that the program or service will achieve the desired change in behavior, knowledge, attitude, skill, or status for participants.

Level I: Single Program

In some cases a librarian may be planning a single program or activity not associated with a series of related programs; in others he or she may have responsibility for only one of a series of programs or may want to assess each program independently. Tables 4-1 through 4-5 are examples of Level I programs with a brief program description, the type of desired outcome, and implications for program planning.

Note that the Fourth of July hat activity (table 4-1) might have multiple outcomes, even though it is a Level I program. The children could also have been given materials to make a colonial hat, for example. The outcome focus might be on developing a skill such as costume hat making, rather than knowledge of hats, which in turn would affect program planning. Which of these outcomes is chosen should not depend solely on a librarian's preference but rather on an assessment of participants and their caregiver needs.

A wide variety of outcomes might also come from the activity shown in table 4-2. But the decision that it is a Level I activity, completed in a single session, helps determine what can be accomplished within the types of outcomes

Table 4-1
Level I: One-Time Activity for a Specific Holiday

Level I program description	Library plans a Fourth of July celebration.
Desired outcome type	Knowledge
Desired outcome	Children learn about hats worn in Colonial America in 1776.
Effect on program planning	Gather age-appropriate history books and pictures of colonial hats to serve as models. Plan a hat identification contest to see if children can demonstrate their newly acquired knowledge.

the participants want. In this case, the skill of matching the duration of a production to the type of planning that has to go into honoring that limitation is the desired result. Deciding this in advance with the knowledge that it fulfills a need or interest of the youth narrows and focuses the planning process.

Table 4-3 illustrates an event that could create confusion among participants because of lack of focus on desired outcomes. This particular program was planned by the Friends of the Library, who paid for an annual author visit. If the desired outcome of the event, which was to encourage children's interest

Table 4-2
Level I: Single Session of an Anticipated New Program Run as a Pilot

Level I program description	Video production experience for upper elementary students
Desired outcome type	Skill
Desired outcome	Students can make a 30-second commercial about a school or community program of their choice.
Effect on program planning	Prepare to demonstrate a video project that can be accomplished in a set period of time and explain why it qualifies as such. Design activities that allow evaluation of studentsí new skills.

Table 4-3
Level I: Celebrity Invited to the Library

Level I program description	Friends of the Library invite an author/illustrator to an event open to community parents and children. The author talks about a treed environment and gives parents and children projects to do together.
Desired outcome type	Attitude
Desired outcome	Young children gain respect for forest environments.
Effect on program planning	In addition to the usual other books by an author included in an author visit, gather books that emphasize care for the environment; include books that suggest family activities with this emphasis. Include stories about the animals and environmental themes mentioned in the visiting author's featured book.

in their community's outdoor environment, had not been communicated to both the author and the library staff, the experience would have lacked focus for the participants. In such circumstances, the outcome might not be achieved. The author might have talked about her books on a different theme, or the librarians might have provided resources on a different topic.

Librarians visiting a day-care center, shown in table 4-4, might have several desired outcomes, including an emphasis on emergent literacy. But previous conversation with this day-care center's program planning team, including parents, had focused the librarians on the outcome of interesting children and their parents in coming to the library. Since this was a Level I activity, expectations for the outcomes had to be quite specific. Sometimes change in or impact on behavior is easier to measure than other types of changes or outcomes.

Sometimes library displays are created simply because the library staff is committed to a topic, such as intellectual freedom in the table 4-5 example. But what if a desired outcome is associated with a targeted group of youth, such as teens? And what if a teen advisory board has identified that outcome? Librarians can plan an activity that matches the level of effort, in this case Level I, as a quick check, or "instant evaluation" (discussed in chapter 10), to determine whether the outcome is achieved, at least in the short term.

For beginners with OBPE, focusing on a single session may be a good way to gain experience, to start the process. A trial run on a smaller basis sometimes clears the way for a more concerted or longer-term effort. It is better to start small and succeed than to "use a lot to say a little." Many of these single programs or services could well be nested within larger library efforts (a "get a card campaign" or series of anticensorship programs), but the youth librarian does not have to take on the entire project or the large-scale evaluation. Focus is the word of the day.

Table 4-4
Level I: Library Staff Visit to a Community Agency

Level I program description	Library staff visits a community center to join an after-school activity to encourage young children and their parents to use the library.
Desired outcome type	Behavior
Desired outcome	Children obtain a library card to encourage them to become regular library users.
Effect on program planning	Bring library card sign-up forms that parents can obtain when they pick up their children. Arrange with the staff for a follow-up visit to the library.

Table 4-5
Level III: Display with Specific Theme, Purpose

Level I program description	During Banned Books Week a display is placed at the entrance to the young adult section.
Desired outcome type	Attitude
Desired outcome	Young readers develop an appreciation for the wide reach and futility of censorship.
Effect on program planning	Incorporate some kind of activity, e.g., a large poster that asks those entering to make a comment about a banned book they have read. Consider how to encourage participation and what to do with requests to check out the books on display.

Level II: Groups of Programs on a Common Topic or Theme

Rather than launch a series of programs or a major project, a library may plan a more modest, limited-term intervention that is nonetheless more complex than a single-activity Level I program or service.

Series of programs centered on a theme are common in many libraries. But the desired outcomes of these programs are not always clear. The Black History Month example (table 4-6) demonstrates how one desired outcome can affect planning for an entire series. Without knowledge of the desired outcome, this decision might be made around other issues, such as convenience of the library staff to execute the program in a particular manner. Although such practical matters must be considered, they are not the primary factor when a specific change is targeted.

Increased teen reading or continuation of reading skills during the summer might be the desired outcome of a series of programs, as in table 4-7. But building a teen community might go unnoticed if the outcomes are not developed with the input of the targeted participants. In the St. Louis Public Library, youth who participated in focus groups mentioned again and again the desire to share knowledge, whether about computers, books, music, or websites, and whether online or in person. So wise librarians, if they have gathered this information, will consider this outcome when planning a series of programs, making it more relevant to the user group and more likely to achieve the desired outcome.

Table 4-6
Level II: Series of Programs Celebrates a National Event

Level II program description	For Black History Month, the childrenś room holds some activity each Saturday related to African American history. This series may be part of the libraryś general efforts to achieve the outcome of greater awareness and appreciation of library users for the contributions of persons from various racial or ethnic groups to American society. The childrenś librarian may be responsible only for planning and assessing the outcomes of this particular series of programs.
Desired outcome type	Knowledge
Desired outcome	Children attending the programs know about African American history in the 1950s and 1960s.
Effect on program planning	Decide which elements of this phase of history to include in the sessions and how to divide up the material among the sessions to achieve a satisfactory outcome.

Table 4-7
Level II: Multiweek Series of Programs Aimed at a Specific Group of Youth

Level II program description	Summer read-a-thon for teens is planned with weekly activities for six weeks.
Desired outcome type	Behavior
Desired outcome	Teens form a cohesive reading community.
Effect on program planning	Plan activities to emphasize not only reading but also teen responsibility, interdependence, and interactivity.

Babysitting skills are important to many young teens (table 4-8). Sometimes they are crucial, as when teens are taking care of a younger sibling on a daily basis. But the specific desired outcomes, and whether they are knowledge, skill, behavior, or attitude, must be identified, for the program cannot provide them all. The most important outcomes vary from community to community.

Table 4-8
Level II: Series of Programs to Increase Competence in Typical Young Teen Jobs

Level II program description	Library staff plans a series of child-care programs for young teen babysitters.
Desired outcome type	Skill
Desired outcome	Participants can take care of a baby using proper health and safety measures.
Effect on program planning	Secure equipment necessary for teen demonstration. Think about how to demonstrate strategies for babies with various temperaments. Incorporate safety tips. Get advice from expert.

A good example of a program appropriate for Level II OBPE but part of a Level III effort is Club Tech, one of the Project CATE programs (table 4-9). Club Tech consisted of a series of ten weekly sessions for kids in grades 6–8, each with the goal of helping participants develop a specific computer-related skill. The outcomes in table 4-9 are for individual Level I activities. The Level II outcome is kids better equipped to use the computer in a variety of ways. Of course, Club Tech was only one small component of Project CATE, which was designed to plan for and evaluate the use of computers by youth ages nine through thirteen.

Each Club Tech session involved a different program activity. The staff evaluated each session separately (as in a Level I program), but the evaluations were used to modify future sessions and as part of the cumulative assessment of the entire series. More about this type of evaluation is discussed in chapter 10.

The development of Club Tech to meet desired outcomes is described in chapter 9. The input of stakeholders was essential in developing this program. Assessing the impact of individual components or the entire series of technology-related activities provided important information to the Club Tech staff about how to implement another series of Club Tech activities. The library staff associated with Club Tech was responsible for planning and assessing the outcomes of this activity but were not asked to assess the impact of the entire technology program.

Table 4-9
Level II: Club Tech Description of Activities and Outcomes

Week	Program Title	Type of Program or Activity	Desired Outcome Type	Desired Level II Outcome
1	Learn to Keyboard	Keyboarding instruction and games	Skill	Participants can perform basic keyboarding techniques.
2	Create a Poster	Creating an event poster with text and clip art	Skill	Participants can use basic functions of Microsoft Word.
3	Write a Review	Finding examples of music and video reviews on Internet and creating own review offline	Skill	Participants know how to locate specific items on Internet and can use Microsoft Word to create a document.
4	Scavenger Hunt	Online scavenger hunt to locate Internet "treasures"	Skill	Participants can use the Internet to answer factual research questions.
5	Computer Music	Using online synthesizers to create music	Skill	Participants can locate and use various types of online music makers.
6	Create a Web Page	Creating a web page using basic HTML	Skill	Participants can use online tools to create a web page.
7	All About Me	Producing an autobiographical presentation using PowerPoint	Skill	Participants can use Microsoft PowerPoint to create a presentation.
8	Family Tree	Using PowerPoint to create a family tree	Skill	Participants can use Microsoft PowerPoint as both a presentation and an organizational tool.
9	Graphing in Excel	Making a graph with Excel	Skill	Participants can use a database program to create a graph.
10	Word Search	Creating a word search with Excel	Skill	Participants can use a database program to create a word search.

Level III: Multifaceted Program Planning and Evaluation

Each of the following Level III efforts and many others like them are likely to consist of several individual components, yet guidance is needed for the overall desired outcomes. Each is likely to have multiple stakeholders whose opinions are valuable to the library in its planning and evaluation. Project CATE is an example of just such a multifaceted program with a variety of stakeholders, some with different expectations that had to be reconciled in the development of expected outcomes.

A project that aims at a particular age group over a span of two years, such as in table 4-10, would by necessity be multifaceted and include several programs and services. Perhaps it is clear that an outcome stated for a project of this magnitude would have to be supported with Level I and Level II programs and services, with the involvement of individual staff members varying.

The programs and services shown in table 4-11 involved not only the participants for whom the outcomes were planned but community stakeholders as well. As in Project CATE, the outcomes were developed and assessed with contributions from all who had a stake in the desired changes. Careful, detailed, and long-term OBPE was called for.

Table 4-12 shows a simple expression of Project CATE at Level III. The listed outcome, of course, is only one of many possible choices at this level.

The multifaceted project shown in table 4-13 comes from a real collaborative partnership between a museum and a library. Unique and innovative programs and services particularly benefit from the CATE OBPE process because the documented desired outcomes and carefully worked-out plans to achieve them serve to convince those who may doubt the wisdom of such an endeavor.

Table 4-10
Level III: Substantial Addition to and Change of Scope of an Existing Service

Level III program description	Library launches an enhanced service for very young children, e.g., additional programs and services for children from birth to two years.
Desired outcome type	Attitude
Desired outcome	By age two, children perceive the public library as a desirable place to be.
Effect on program planning	Develop strategies to encourage repeat visits by this age group and their caretakers.

Table 4-11
Level III: Configuration of Programs and Services for a Targeted
Population—English as Second Language

Level III program description	Library plans a series of services and opportunities for youth for whom English is a second language.
Desired outcome type	Behavior
Desired outcome	Those for whom English is a second language take advantage of community resources.
Effect on program planning	Incorporate appearances of persons from community agencies into literacy sessions.

Table 4-12
Level III: Configuration of Programs and Services for a Targeted Population—
Project CATE

Level III program description	Library undertakes a major new initiative: technology services for middle school students.
Desired outcome type	Skill
Desired outcome	Participants will search successfully for online information.
Effect on program planning	Include ways to develop this skill in the programming, including introduction to search engines and how to use them.

Table 4-13
Level III: Preparation for a Major Fiscal Project

Level III program description	Library plans for construction of a new children's room in cooperation with the community science museum.
Desired outcome type	Knowledge
Desired outcome	Children learn science by simply being in the museum-library thanks to the unique organization of materials.
Effect on program planning	Demonstrate to donors that children will learn science better through this unusual arrangement.

■ ■ ■

No other models of outcome-based evalution of which we are aware provide guidance to librarians on how to adjust the level of planning and evaluation to match the intended program or service. This is one of the several unusual features of the CATE OBPE model and one that makes it attractive to busy professionals. As the CATE OBPE model is described in the rest of this book, reference is made to factors relevant to different levels of effort. By the end of the book, you should be able to choose an area in which to develop an OBPE, identify the level of effort required, and feel confident about how to proceed with your own planning and evaluation efforts. And like Tock in *The Phantom Tollbooth*, you will know never to use a lot to accomplish a little.

Five

Developing an Outcome-Based Planning and Evaluation Project

There are several "homework" assignments to do before beginning to use OBPE. Some time and effort spent before actually starting an outcome-based project will save problems as the evaluation progresses. First, the youth services planner must decide what project or services need to be evaluated and at what level of OBPE, then several activities are needed before the OBPE process is begun.

The project manager has to develop support for the specific OBPE project from library administration, the youth services staff, and library staff from other departments. If there is a positive culture of evaluation in the library, outcome setting and measuring will easily become a normal part of providing service and using outcome evaluation results an essential part of library planning. If the library does not evaluate programs and services and rarely asks for user input, OBPE may be more difficult to implement simply because it is new or different from common practice.

When electing to use OBPE, youth services managers should see if other libraries have had success with outcome evaluation in similar situations. This would including reading published materials as well as searching for grant reports, library annual reports, or individual library reports that outline types of data collection, data analysis, and evaluation results. Checking for information on prior evaluations with neighboring libraries and from consultants at library systems or the state library can shape the best OBPE project designs and help avoid repeating the mistakes of others. Checking to see what evaluation and planning techniques have been used within one's own library may also give some direction for planning the next OBPE project.

Each OBPE project should have a specific manager or leader, one who is clear about staff assignments and can identify areas for staff training. The project manager should create a planning "plan" that includes a clear description of the project, a timetable, a budget, and project assignments for key staff.

If data are to be collected from children and adults, the library should have a statement on gathering and using human subject information. If schools or other non-library institutions are cooperating in the project, there should be a letter of agreement from the appropriate external administrator. And, of course, the youth services manager should get formal permission for the project from the library director or library board.

Selecting an OBPE Project

Because libraries differ, each youth services manager must select and define the program or service to study using OBPE. The youth services department may begin to use outcome-based evaluation because the whole library is involved in evaluation. In this case, the scope and subject of evaluation may be assigned and the youth services staff will select activities of importance within this assignment. Or, if the youth services department is the only department using outcome evaluation, it will have to focus on projects that are simple and understandable as it gets started.

As Durrance and Fisher (2005, 33) point out, librarians have hunches about how their services impact library users. OBPE helps focus and validate these hunches, but care is needed when selecting a project (and level) and designing it once the subject of study is selected. The "how tos" are addressed in the rest of this book, but the first step is to select what to study.

Since outcome-based evaluation involves measuring what patrons know, do, or believe, start with answering the following questions:

1. *What program or service do we want to know more about?* This could be a program that is not going as well as you would like, one you want to start to use, or one that needs redesign to serve more of a particular target audience. You may need to know more about the consequences of dropping a program or service. Often librarians select programs or services to study that need changes. Some librarians look at programs that have not been changed for years, to find out if the tradition still serves the needs of today's children.

2. *What questions need answers?* Why do you want to change the program you have selected? What questions do other staff members have about this program? Have users asked questions about this program? Write down all possible questions, group similar questions, and select the most important ones to study.

3. *What specifically about the program or service can be measured?* You may be interested in services to preschoolers and decide to evaluate outreach to Head Start, using your parenting collection, but not to evaluate preschool story time. You must decide what questions you have and what evaluations will answer them.

4. *What audiences will be involved in this study?* If you are interested in teens, you must involve teens and perhaps their parents and teachers in the study. Are there ways to get information from these groups? Do you have access to these groups? Think about special problems in communicating with these groups and how to solve them. You may be interested in immigrant families, so you may need non-English speakers' help in the project. Young children who do not read cannot fill out a written survey, so parents or teachers may be needed to communicate with young children and help gather information on their interests.

5. *What will you do with the information you gather?* Think about what should be done with both positive and negative results.

It may take a few days or weeks, or even several months, to answer these questions and select and describe the subject of the OBPE study. Involve staff, including library administration, and talk informally with library users. Check with colleagues in other libraries to hone ideas and develop the OBPE project. Consider what level of project is practical and comfortable. Pick a project that will help you to do a better job. Select a project consistent with issues being addressed by the library as a whole. Understand that the library can do a series of OBPE projects and that one project will not answer all questions.

Developing a Culture of Evaluation

For libraries that have a history of institutional planning and goal setting, the use of the CATE OBPE model is a natural next step. If the youth services staff has actively and systematically evaluated programs and services, OBPE provides a further way to manage an evaluation project and use its results. If, however, evaluation and planning are new to the library or to youth services, it is important for staff, administrators, and library board to understand the benefits of outcome-based planning before the start of a particular project. If evaluation is considered unimportant or simply a way of meeting external demands for accountability with the least possible impact on the library, that library is probably not ready to commit to a major OBPE project.

The point of evaluation is to gather data and draw conclusions about the level of success of the program or service being evaluated. After understanding the conclusions drawn from the data, the library staff should be willing to make changes that will improve success from the users' point of view. If a library is not ready to accept evaluation results, or make changes suggested by those results, there are some things to do before launching a major OBPE project.

Starting OBPE with a Level I evaluation (see chapter 4) could help staff members feel comfortable with an evaluation and learn from it, particularly if the program evaluated is one the staff has selected. Starting with small, simple evaluations can build respect for using evaluation as well as skills needed to do evaluation. For example, if a staff wants better information on upcoming homework assignments from local teachers, it may be willing to survey teachers on their use of the library's homework alert system. Results of this survey could help the library change the system of homework alerts to make it more attractive to teachers. By using a follow-up discussion with the whole library staff, everyone will gain a better idea of why the evaluation was done, what was learned, and how the service was improved.

Another way to develop a culture of evaluation is to ask for and use staff opinions to plan programs and services. Although most managers solicit staff opinions informally, a good way to get staff members to accept more formal evaluation is to do a more formal questionnaire to gather staff opinions on future programs. The staff may offer opinions on themes for summer reading programs, on which staff training is the highest priority, or on the most useful databases to purchase. Libraries are not run by the vote of their employees, but some decisions can be made on the basis of staff preferences and expertise. By participating in surveys and seeing how gathering information can inform decision making, employees experience the value of evaluation firsthand.

Using outside consultants to help train staff about the value of OBPE and sharing examples of evaluations that helped other libraries improve services and gain funding can help a library appreciate the value of systematic evaluation. Many professional associations offer workshops on planning, outcomes, and evaluation. Sending several staff members to such workshops builds respect for evaluation and acceptance that it is the norm for public libraries. Talking or reading about how other libraries use evaluation can make evaluation more attractive and interesting to a staff that has limited experience with it.

When Project CATE was being planned, the St. Louis Public Library staff already had experience gathering and using patron opinions. The library had used focus groups of both adults and children to get community input before branch renovations. Teachers and parents had been surveyed and interviewed to evaluate the library's early reading services, and library users had participated in several phone interviews to help the library board decide to put a tax increase proposal up for a vote of St. Louis citizens. Because library leaders expected to base decisions, at least in part, on patron evaluation and opinions, developing an outcome evaluation model was supported. Library staff members understood the importance of outcome planning, so there was little resistance to using OBPE.

Although some libraries have less experience with outcome evaluation, it is important to set up each OBPE project for success by making sure the library leadership will value the information collected and use it to plan future services and programs. A positive attitude toward evaluation is a precursor to success with OPBE.

Gathering Information

Although outcome-based evaluation is a fairly recent introduction to libraries, many of the component evaluative techniques have been used and reported by libraries for years. It is useful to know how other libraries have used surveys, focus groups, interviews, and observation to understand user needs and preferences. One of the strengths of OBPE is that it focuses on local views of the library, but it is still helpful to learn as much as is practical about other libraries' experiences before beginning any particular project. As suggested in chapter 2, many non-library agencies have used outcome-based planning, so checking not-for-profit literature and websites also helps library project managers broaden their knowledge of outcome planning.

It is also a good practice to check the library's archives or official files to review its previous evaluation projects. Obviously, this is especially important if staff responsible for an OBPE project are new to the library. Previous plans and results of past surveys will put OBPE in context locally and help decisions as it proceeds. Sharing summaries or the best of the information found during a literature search with library administration and staff is a good way to gain support for an OBPE project.

Creating an OBPE Plan

If OBPE is being used as part of a grant, then the practical issues have been described in the grant proposal. In this case the proposal can be the draft of the

OBPE plan. As the project beginning gets closer, the plan must become more specific. Typically an OBPE plan should include an abstract of the project (a brief description of why the project is being done and main elements of the project); the questions OBPE will answer and how data will be collected; which staff members will be involved and in what roles; cooperating institutions (schools, Scout groups, after-school programs, etc.) and their roles in the project; and a project timetable and budget.

The abstract can be a short paragraph, such as "We will ask children attending Club Tech meetings what they have learned at a meeting and what topics should be covered to get ideas for topics of future Club meetings." Or it can be several paragraphs that give the what, why, when, and who of an evaluation project. This description should summarize the important facts of the project as if describing it to someone who understands the library but is just learning about the project; include goals of the service or program.

Next, the service or program to be evaluated should be described in such a way that the kinds of information to be gathered from children and other stakeholders are identified. For example, focus might be specifically on a library's technology services rather than on all its services. To understand how to develop the program (or change a current program), it will be important to ask children about their access to computers, their attitudes toward computers, their knowledge of computers, and perhaps also how they use the library's computers. Every project will address questions that best fit that project, including priorities of the library and practical issues such as how many questions can be addressed at a time and what information is possible to collect from and about the children using the library.

When questions have been identified, then the plan should include how the questions will be answered and how the answers will be reported. The questions mentioned above might be answered by a short survey at the end of the program. Then the children's answers could be tallied and reported to library staff and administration in a short report.

The OBPE plan should identify who will be involved, what each person will do, and about how much time participation will take. A project leader should be identified, so everyone in the library understands who has authority to ask for help and who answers questions as the project progresses. This part of the OBPE plan should include people associated with the library, primarily staff, but also volunteers and outside consultants if appropriate. If people from other organizations (teachers, social workers, day-care staff, Scout leaders) have parts in the project, their roles should be described. Information about library user (children, parents, caregivers) involvement should be included; this might be as simple as stating that the teen librarian will create a program evaluation to be reviewed by the library director and given to children attending the library's Club Tech program. Creating the survey may take half an hour, including review, and children can complete it in five minutes. For more involved projects, a person may be hired to direct the program, with several staff members having work assignments.

If teachers (or other child-serving adults) are going to bring children to the library, host librarian visits, or participate in focus groups or be interviewed, then these activities should be described. Each outside agency has rules about cooperation, and these must be respected. Some schools allow libraries to contact teachers directly, leaving participation up to individual teachers. Other districts require school administrative approval for cooperative projects. If the latter case, the OBPE plan should identify the contact person at the school district. It is helpful to plan how outside people will be recruited and selected for participation.

The last section of the OBPE plan should include a project budget and timeline. If the staff can manage the project in addition to its other duties, then the cost of this can be disregarded, but the cost of any extra staff hired for the project must be listed in the OBPE budget. In the same way, if other costs such as printing surveys or extra flyers are to be covered by the library's regular budget, then they need not be included. It is important to keep the budget and timetable simple, but it is equally important to anticipate the extra costs of doing OBPE as well as to leave enough time to get the project completed.

The simpler the OBPE project, the simpler the project plan. A Level I plan may be a few paragraphs included in a monthly report, whereas a Level III plan may be several pages long. In any project, the plan helps all parties agree to the project before the work is begun and is a basis from which to agree on changes as they are needed during the project.

Another preparatory task is to confirm that the OBPE project fits within the library's established policies and procedures. Since confidentiality of patron information and other library records is likely addressed in policy, it is important to know what is and is not allowed before beginning the project. Most libraries ask users for opinions about library programs and services and consider this a part of the regular operation of the library. If the OBPE involves patron records (e.g., circulation, computer use), there should be specific ways for the required confidentiality to be maintained and for users to decline to participate. Any user who participates in evaluation of the library or provides information should give informed consent; that is, they should know what is being evaluated, why their opinions are being sought, and how their information will be used.

In most locations, children need parental permission to participate in any extraordinary evaluation study; that is, the parent or guardian rather than the child gives informed consent. At the St. Louis Public Library, children filled out program evaluations and voluntarily answered questions about how they used the library as part of the library's ordinary responsibility of getting input from the public. Children could (and did) decline to participate, and no individual names were connected to specific information in summaries or reports. When children participated in focus groups, a parent permission slip was required, since a video was taken in which children were identified by name. The video was viewed only by staff, and written reports did not use the children's names, so identities were kept confidential. Each library must sort out and define the line between "ordinary" library business and activities that need parent permission.

Once the OBPE project manager has helped the library understand and value evaluation, written an OBPE project plan, and decided how to work with the library's human subject policies, it is time to get formal approval of the project. Again practices differ from library to library, and Level I projects may not need specific acknowledgment or approval for each program evaluation. But no library administrator likes to be surprised by evaluations being undertaken; the project manager needs to be assured of cooperation from library staff and the budget to move forward.

In some libraries, plans for OBPE projects are approved by the library's board, and in others by the library's director. In either case, the project is not ready to begin until permission has been given. For Level III projects, the library administration should be involved in the planning stage and will have valuable insights about how best to complete the project. In larger libraries, department heads and other administrators may need to agree to projects even if the majority of work will be done by the youth services staff, so these key individuals must be involved in the planning stage. The wise youth services manager will also have a plan for communicating progress to the library administration during the project.

■ ■ ■

Like doing stretching exercises before running, warm-up planning for OBPE makes the process smoother and the findings more useful. Many factors dictate how elaborate the warm-up need be. Generally, planning for Level I projects is short and simple, but still worth the effort. Taking a half hour to plan how to best evaluate a specific program makes the actual evaluation go smoothly and helps the staff and participants understand what is being done and how it will improve library service. Level II and Level III projects need more preparation time and effort. The more people (including both staff and public), time, and money being used for an OBPE, the more careful the preparations must be. Although the main decisions involved in an OBPE project relate to collecting and analyzing data, articulating outcomes, and designing and measuring the impact of programs and services, a little pre-planning goes a long way to ensure the success of OBPE. How to design and conduct an OBPE are addressed in the following chapters, but pre-planning is essential to success.

PART III

Using the CATE Outcome-Based Planning and Evaluation Model

Six

Phase I

Gathering Information: Types

With this chapter we begin an in-depth discussion of how to apply the CATE OBPE model by concentrating on Phase I. In Phase I, information is gathered that will be used to determine

- what kinds of programs and services are needed
- what outcomes to target in the design and development of programs and services

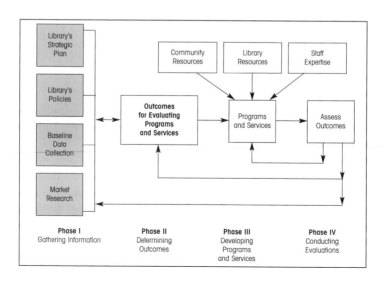

■ what types of evaluation strategies best assess the extent to which the desired outcomes are achieved

The information gathering process utilizes both existing data, including data already collected by the library or other sources, and information to be collected from stakeholders. This combination of data sources is used to construct a comprehensive picture of the intersection between the library and the community it serves as a basis for program and service development. Gathering this data ensures that program and service development is realistic in terms of the mission and resources of the library, relevant to user needs, and likely to have the impact the targeted user group and other stakeholders have identified as desirable.

Phase I outlines four types of information needed to support the other phases of the CATE OBPE model: the library's strategic plan, the library's policies, baseline data collection, and market research. In this chapter we discuss these types of information and how they contribute to OBPE. Specific methods for gathering information from existing sources and from people are covered in chapter 7.

The Library's Strategic Plan

The library's strategic plan is the best source for information about how the library sees itself in the context of its defined service area and what it hopes to achieve during the current planning cycle. Ideally, goals for the youth department make sense in terms of the larger goals of the library. Placing plans for youth services within a larger coordinated effort that takes advantage of the library's strengths and strategic planning process helps ensure support for new initiatives and allows all areas of the library to work together efficiently.

If there is no strategic plan, or if planning is new, it is important that the youth department be a full participant when committees begin strategic planning. Services for youth, like other library services, must be represented in the library's overall strategic plan. Further, the integration of programs and services for youth into the plan developed for the whole library is critical to their success. Including youth services in the strategic planning process is important to ensure that there is commitment and support for youth and that these services are integrated into the library's general effort to serve the information needs of the community.

In the absence of formal planning, or plans to plan, youth services must take on the effort required to understand the place of the library in the community and the information needs of the youth the library serves. Sources of help in this endeavor include university research institutes, state library agencies, and professional library consultants.

A strategic plan typically has key elements that are important to understand before undertaking any program or service development. A review of the strategic plan provides important data about the library's place in the community and its commitment to providing responsive programs and services. Particularly informative are the vision and mission statements; the identification of strengths, weaknesses, opportunities, and threats (SWOTs) developed during planning; community needs analyses; adoption of service roles; and formal statements of the library's goals and objectives for the current planning cycle.

Vision and Mission Statements

Vision and mission statements are a cornerstone of the strategic planning process. The vision statement is an expression of the place the library hopes to achieve in the life of the community in broad terms. The Chula Vista Public Library provides one example: "The Chula Vista Library is the community's family room where reading and learning are encouraged and celebrated" (Chula Vista Public Library 2005).

The mission statement expresses the business of the library in terms of whom it serves, how, and why, for example, "The St. Louis Public Library will provide learning resources and information services that support and improve individual, family, and community life" (St. Louis Public Library, n. d.).

The value of vision and mission statements is that they provide a clear picture of what both the community and employees of the library should expect in terms of priorities for service and resource allocation. Initiatives from the community or within the library that fall within the scope of the library's vision and mission are excellent candidates for development.

SWOTs

One feature of library strategic planning that sets it apart from other long-range planning is the identification and analysis of the library in the context of the community. This process makes explicit not only the strengths and weakness of the library as an organization but also the opportunities and threats it faces. The collection and interpretation of SWOTs are central to strategic planning.

One example of a strength identified by the St. Louis Public Library during Project CATE was its relationship with the community, which sees the library as an important service provider worthy of support. One perceived weakness was the lack of technological skills among the general staff. One opportunity was a history of good working relationships with the local schools. One threat was the possibility of the community seeing the library as the solution to many of its challenges, thus spreading library resources too thin to have a real impact in areas directly related to its vision and mission.

Programs and services that take a SWOT analysis seriously take advantage of the library's assets and do a better job of making the most of what the library has to offer the community.

Community Needs Analyses

The community needs analysis normally contains information on the composition of the community, identified user information needs, and an assessment of which needs the library is best suited to address. These understandings include information such as gender, age, ethnicity, and socioeconomic and education levels. It is also important to know what information organizations, other than the library, are available in the community. For Project CATE, it was important to know where youth in St. Louis went to use computers. Did they have access at home, at school, or at other locations such as a parent's workplace, friend's house, or church?

Not only does the community analysis provide a sound overview of whom the library serves in a general sense, it may also provide insight into the needs of specific user groups and library responses they might find useful. Understanding the user community, who they are and what they want from the library, is basic to the development of programs and services responsive to user needs. This understanding should include a picture of the community in general and of specific user groups, such as youth, which are the audience of interest for a specific project. In addition to demographic information, it can be useful to know what kinds of information resources are preferred, for what purposes, and the circumstances that lead users to seek information and access library programs and services.

Service Roles

Service roles, or responses, further describe what the library wants to do and for whom during the current planning cycle. Service roles support the library's mission statement by further specifying the types of service the library sees as its priority and communicating this decision to both the public and library staff.

The number of potential service role types described in the literature has grown from eight in 1987 (McClure et al. 1987) to a current thirteen (Himmel and Wilson 1998; Nelson 2001). Whereas the original eight service roles included "The Children's Door to Learning," the current thirteen described in the literature are more general and do not specify the needs of youth. However, Walter (1992) interprets all eight original roles in terms of their application to the provision of library service to youth.

The St. Louis Public Library provides an example of the relationship between service roles and vision and mission statements. One service role that makes sense in terms of the library's aim "to provide learning resources and information services that support and improve individual, family, and community life" is the role of lifelong learning. Adopting this role means that the library wants to help "address the desire for self-directed personal growth and development opportunities" (Nelson 2001). To do this, the library is developing programs and services on a wide range of topics, including special topics of local interest. In programming for youth, this can mean providing programs targeted to topics of current interest, such as graphic novels or computers. It can also mean ensuring that a wide variety of materials in a variety of formats is available to respond to children's self-generated needs and questions stemming from real-life situations such as starting a hobby, getting a new pet, the first day at school, and puberty.

Just as youth services must make sense in terms of the library's mission statement, they must also support the service roles the library has adopted for the current planning cycle. In cases where youth services are seen as having their own mission and roles, these should be stated explicitly and used to guide program and service development.

Goals and Objectives

The goals and objectives developed during the planning process are essential because they are the basis for later evaluation. Just as the service roles further clarify the library's intent, the goals and objectives work to make these intentions both concrete and measurable. Goals express the condition the library is working toward in this planning cycle. Objectives provide statements of specified, measurable results the library is committed to achieving within a defined timeframe. For example, a goal might be that children in a service area are prepared for school when they enter kindergarten. A related objective might be to incorporate early literacy skills training into 100 percent of storytime programs provided for preschool age children over the next calendar year. When objectives are stated in ways that provide measurable goals, outline activities that reflect a reasonable expectation for staff, and have a clear due date, they provide a concrete framework not only for meeting the library's goals and objectives but also for evaluating success.

The CATE OBPE model advocates the development of outcome-based goals and objectives as an extension of the library's strategic planning process. Thinking about and defining the library's goals in terms of the desired impact on the community ensure that this dimension of service is not overlooked, that it is described in measurable terms, and that it becomes an integral part of program and service evaluation. Other projects have demonstrated the possibility of determining outcomes of library services after the fact; a key feature of the CATE OBPE model is that it addresses the question of impact up-front and makes it a guiding factor in the activities the library undertakes. This makes it possible to include all stakeholders in the conversation about what desired outcomes should be and to measure progress toward desired outcomes during the design, development, and implementation phases as well as later when assessing the extent to which established programs and services are meeting goals.

For libraries that are already using the CATE OBPE model or other outcome-based techniques, this step may already be in place. If not, data must be collected to identify the desired outcomes. Remember that planning is cyclical and that communities change. In different planning cycles, the library may see its role in the community differently. For this reason, the CATE OBPE model revisits Phase I periodically to determine if changes in the community, the library's position in the community, or resources available to the library require an adjustment in the vision, mission, and service roles of the library. Just as the library's service emphasis may change over time, outcomes targeted in a previous planning cycle may no longer be pertinent to the user and must be reassessed in each planning cycle to remain responsive to community needs.

The Library's Policies

Policies are rules established to provide guiding principles that inform procedures, guidelines, and decision making regarding the functions of the library. Library policies are an important input in understanding the framework within which programs and services for youth are designed, developed, and delivered. Many factors shape the development of library policy, which in turn influences how library work is done. For instance, library policy can be influenced by federal legislation, professional standards (e.g., as explicated by the ALA), as well as state and local government and community standards. One example of library policy affected by federal legislation is the Children's Internet Protection Act, which mandates the use of technology to filter Internet content accessible to youth in libraries that receive federal funding.

The library's policy manual is the natural place to go to review policies that may influence project planning or to identify policies that need reassessment in response to changing needs. If the library does not have a policy manual, it may be necessary to collect policies from various sources including written and electronic documentation. Youth services may have its own collection development and acceptable use policies, and this documentation must not be overlooked.

Nelson and Garcia suggest that public libraries typically have at least five policy types: public service, technical services, personnel, financial, and collection development. They further divide public service policy into six categories: governance and organizational structure, management, customer services, circulation services, information services, and group services (2003, 24, 27). These types and categories provide a good starting place for thinking through which policies are pertinent to project plans. As relevant library policies are identified, collected, and reviewed, one should consider not only the impact of existing policy on project plans but also the impact of the project on current policy. Have conditions changed in ways that require policy changes? Will new developments require new policies to keep up with the times?

In dealing with technology, Project CATE required sensitivity to pending legislation regarding filters and their impact on existing library policy, which supports equal access to children in the library. The project also prompted discussion of needed changes in library policy concerning the number of users per computer and the need for library cards by those accessing library computers.

Baseline Data Collection

The collection of baseline data provides an understanding of current use before new programs and services are implemented. This is important, because without an idea of what current use looks like, it is difficult to demonstrate the effect of new programs and services. The need for data collection depends on factors such as whether the library is already collecting data about use and whether the data collected are relevant to the evaluation of new programs and services. For instance, if the library is developing a service to promote the circulation of storytime kits, circulation data already available may provide a point of comparison after the implementation of the new service. In this case, no new data would need to be collected. If, instead, the library wants to change how children are using computers, but computer use has not been measured previously, it is important to collect such data to be able to measure changes in use after the implementation of the new program or service. Methods for collecting data are discussed in chapter 7.

In the CATE OBPE model, the collection of baseline data includes gathering the opinions of stakeholders about desired outcomes for library programs and services. In particular, CATE OBPE includes the voices of youth. Other potentially important stakeholders are parents, teachers, community leaders, librarians, and school library media specialists. Which stakeholders are important varies depending on the program or service under consideration.

Market Research

Marketing—"a cyclical process designed to allow organizations to allocate resources and design programs strategically to meet user needs" (Lee 2003, 186)—shares many of the qualities and methods used in strategic planning. Like strategic planning, marketing is based on the development of vision and mission statements, an understanding of the organization and its competition, and knowledge of users both in a demographic sense and in terms of their needs and the types of programs and services likely to meet these needs effectively. As discussed here, marketing research is a general set of guidelines, plans, and other tools to develop awareness of items that should be considered during the various stages of a CATE OBPE project. Just as a library would not develop a full strategic plan to conduct a Level I project, a library would not develop a comprehensive marketing research plan for a limited-effort development. It is, however, possible that even a Level I project will reveal inadequacies in and opportunities for refining and further developing the library's existing marketing plan.

The first goal of marketing research is user satisfaction and recognition of the opportunities to respond to user needs in ways that make sense in terms of the library's strategic plan. The market research done in Phase I of the CATE OBPE model is designed to provide data for responding to user needs as the outcomes are developed in Phase II. Marketing prompts another set of activities that support the library's efforts to meet its goals and objectives.

A second goal of market research is to develop a strategy for responding to opportunities that optimize the provision of programs and services. This goal involves considering what are commonly called the Four Ps: product, price, promotion, and place. Finding the right combination of the Four Ps is the secret to marketing programs and services successfully. Although this marketing strategy should be laid out for all library services, the implementation involving the Four Ps does not occur in Phase I but later, particularly in Phases III and IV. But since CATE OBPE is dynamic, with the various phases interacting, we describe the Four Ps here to lay the groundwork for actions described in other phases.

Of the Four Ps, "product" refers to library programs and services targeted to a specific audience in the service area, such as youth. The central concern here is that both current and proposed programs and services respond to user needs in ways users find appealing. "Price" refers both to the library's costs in providing programs and services and the user's costs in making use of them. For the library, the expense associated with providing programs and services (e.g., staff time, training and resources) compared to the expected benefits is one consideration in decisions about what programs and services to provide. For the user, price may be considered in terms of time, money, and effort. When this price is greater than the user's perception of the value of library programs and services, the success of these programs and services is unlikely.

Increasingly, "place" in libraries refers not only to the physical facility but also to electronic access to resources and services. How, where, and when the user is able to take advantage of programs and services are other factors for success. It is important to deliver programs and services at times and locations that are convenient and meet the lifestyle needs of youth.

"Promotion" is the process of communicating information about programs and services in ways that gain the attention of the target audience. Effective communication, using media and language appropriate to youth, also provides an opportunity to let youth know about the library's role in the community as part of the promotion of programs and services. The use of marketing research in program and service development is further discussed in chapter 9.

A third goal of market research is evaluative. As programs and services are implemented and delivered, it is important to monitor them to ensure that they are having the desired effect. The OBPE model provides a framework that allows the integration of marketing research into the overall planning and evaluation process. This aspect of market research is discussed further in chapter 10.

To meet the first goal of market research, user satisfaction, marketing uses many of the methods seen in strategic planning and the collection of baseline data, such as existing statistics, surveys, focus groups, interviews, and observation. Marketing research also asks many of the same questions as strategic planning, such as who the youth are in the community and what products and services will help them achieve desired outcomes. This means that some of the data needed for a market research analysis may already be available in the library.

Some larger library systems have a marketing department that can be a resource for the marketing aspects of program and service development. Even if there is this kind of expertise in the library, however, it may make sense to hire an outside consultant—specifically, one who specializes in youth. Although the same methods and approaches may be used to research many different user groups, a consultant who understands the youth market knows how to optimize marketing methods with this target audience (McNeal 1999; Siegel, Coffey, and Livingston 2001; Zollo 1999).

■　■　■

As part of reviewing existing documentation, such as the library's strategic plan and policies, in Phase I it is important to determine whether sufficient data exist to support the programs and services under consideration. Does the library know enough about the user to design the programs and services that respond to user needs? Does it know what kinds of outcomes stakeholders see as important for services provided for youth? Are assessments of current programs and services available to provide a point of comparison for future evaluation efforts?

The amount of missing information needed to progress with program and service development is the clearest measure of how much information will need to be gathered to support program development and evaluation. This said, the leveled approach assumes that Level I programs do not require either extensive data collection efforts or extensive evaluation efforts. Major information gathering efforts are normally too intensive in terms of effort and time to take place for each individual program or service or to be performed more often than every three to five years. Once gathered, strategic planning data, library policies, community needs analyses, and so forth feed all levels of program development. Smaller data collection efforts are performed as needed to fill in gaps, supporting continued program development and keeping pace with changes in the community.

Seven

Phase I

Gathering Information: Methods

While it is well and good to understand the different types of information needed to support planning and evaluation, this understanding may be of limited utility unless the "how" of gathering information is also understood. Collecting or even creating documents is easy enough. The collection of baseline data, including information about users that inform the strategic plan and market research, requires more effort and specific skills and expertise. In this chapter we focus on gathering additional information to support planning, development, and evaluation, particularly baseline data collection.

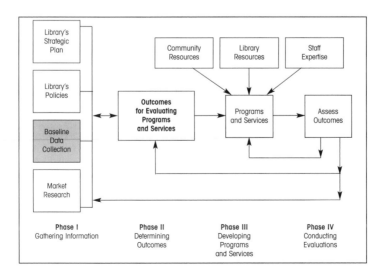

73

To prepare for collecting baseline data, it is important to answer the following questions:

> What does the library need to know that it does not already know in order to support the programs and services under consideration?
>
> What available data sources can provide this information (e.g., documents, records, people)?
>
> What processes (e.g., surveys, focus groups) will be used to collect the data?

Once it is clear what kind of information the library needs, there are many possible ways to collect data that support development and evaluation. For instance, information the library needs is often available free or for a nominal fee. This type of information gathering uses published research, statistics computed by governments or other organizations, and sometimes even the raw data someone else has collected. Other times it is necessary to go directly to the user, potential users, staff, or other stakeholders to gather information. What follows here are descriptions of ways to get information that are commonly used in strategic planning, marketing, developing outcomes, and evaluation.

Using Existing Sources of Information

This type of information gathering uses the work of researchers, government agencies, business and industry, marketing firms, and other organizations to answer questions about the community, user information needs and preferences, cultural factors, and the library's competitors. Existing sources are inexpensive to use and easy to access. Many statistical resources are available in print and on the Web. Electronic indexes have made current library-related literature easier to search, and many articles are available in full text or easily accessible in library collections. The important considerations here are the source of the data, their quality and currency, and why they were originally collected. Make sure the statistics or research used to inform the library's program and service development are from a reputable source. Be aware, though, that even government reports and academic research can be flawed. Be sure to think critically about all resources and assess the quality of the data before incorporating them into any documents or plans.

If the library is considering analyzing raw data collected by someone else, such as survey responses, it is a good idea to examine the questions used in the survey and the intent of the original data collection to ensure that data are useful for the library's purposes. The data will have been collected on the basis of someone else's information needs, and if these needs are not similar to the library's, the information may not be useful and may even be misleading. For example, data collected concerning parents' perceptions of children's technology use can provide only information about what parents think and should not be considered a valid measure of children's perceptions of their technology use or a substitute for studying what children actually do when they use technology. If the library is interested in how children feel about technology or what their skill levels are, it would be better to examine information elicited directly from children who are similar to the children the library is interested in.

Remember that existing sources of data are valuable and should be considered even when the library is planning to collect information directly from users and other stakeholder groups. Existing resources can provide valuable background information for developing questions used to gather additional information from people. The local school district is a good source of information about children in the community. Other local sources include the chamber of commerce, law enforcement groups, realty agencies, museums, businesses, and special interest groups. Existing sources can also help the library identify variables, theories, and approaches that may be valuable in the information gathering process.

Sample Sources

A quick Web search or a visit to the government documents section of the library will reveal the enormous number of sources of statistical data on a library's community, competitors, and users. Data are available at the federal, state, and local levels. Data concerning youth are also available from a variety of foundations and agencies. The following sources are often helpful:

Administration for Children and Families Research and Statistics (http://www.acf.hhs.gov/research.html)

Federal Interagency Forum on Child and Family Statistics (http://www.childstats.gov/)

Child Trends Data Bank (http://www.childtrendsdatabank.org/)

Girl Scouts Statistics and Research on Children, Youth, and Families (http://www.girlscouts.org/research/resources/children_youth_families.asp)

Kids Count census data online, Anne E. Casey Foundation (http://www.aecf.org/kidscount/index.htm)

Library Research Service (http://www.lrs.org/)

National Center for Education Statistics (http://nces.ed.gov/)

Pew Internet & American Life website (http://www.pewinternet.org/)

Statistical Abstract of the United States
(http://www.census.gov/statab/www/)

United States Census (http://www.census.gov/)

United States Census Children
(http://www.census.gov/population/www/socdemo/children.html)

U.S. Department of Education (http://www.ed.gov/index.jhtml)

Many published reports, articles, and books discuss the information needs, preferences, and lifestyles of youth and various subgroups of youth. Youth is a broad category, and depending on the planning project it may need to be broken down. The library may need literature that addresses a specific age or grade range, deals with gender issues in information seeking and provision, or discusses specific cultural or ethnic groups.

Other print-based and electronic resources discuss marketing products and services to youth. The use of marketing in libraries is a growing movement, and numerous resources describe how to use marketing concepts to design, promote, and evaluate library programs and services. Here are a few:

American Library Association. *Marketing Basics*
(http://www.ala.org/ala/pla/plaissues/smartestcardcampaign/
marketingbasics.doc)

McNeal, James U. 1999. *The Kids Market: Myths and Realities*. Ithaca,
NY: Paramount Market Publishing.

Niederlander, Mary. *Marketing Our Libraries On and Off the Internet
Site* (http://www.librarysupportstaff.com/marketinglibs.html)

Ohio Library Council. *Marketing Your Library* (http://www.olc.org/
marketing/)

Zollo, Peter. 1999. *Wise Up to Teens: Insights into Marketing and
Advertising to Teenagers*. 2d ed. Ithaca, NY: New Strategist
Publications.

Example of Use of Existing Research and Statistics

In Project CATE, several sources of existing statistics and research were used to inform the study (Gross, Dresang, and Holt 2004). School district data on reading scores and the number of students per computer in the schools were important to understanding the target audience these programs were meant to reach. Sources such as Kids Count provided demographic data on children in Project CATE, including the number receiving free/reduced lunch, the number living in single-parent households, and the number living in poverty. Existing research helped fill in data on digital divide issues, gender issues, and children's use of technology. Still, since youth and technology in public libraries is a topic about which little is known, a great deal of information had to be gathered directly from users and other stakeholders. This was accomplished by using several methods, including surveys, focus groups, and direct observation.

Gathering Information from People

When gathering information, particularly from young people, it is extremely important to follow standard prescriptions that protect privacy, limit harm, and ensure that participation is voluntary. When data collection from people is funded by the federal government, the agency administering the funds expects adherence to federal regulations concerning the use of human subjects. These regulations are specified on the U.S. Government Printing Office website (http://www.gpoaccess.gov/cfr/index.html), and many universities and other organizations make their institutional review board rules, which are based on the federal guidelines, accessible on the Web as well.

It is standard practice for research conducted by university staff, faculty, and students to be reviewed by the university's review board or human subjects committee and approved before data collection begins. Data collected in schools and school libraries typically require review and permission by the school district. Many public libraries have written standards for data collection that follow the federal rules. In chapter 5 we explained the policies for data collection from users in place at the St. Louis Public Library during Project CATE. Standards may include informed consent forms and other useful documents as well. If a public library does not have its own guidelines for data collection, guidelines may be available at the city or county office to which the library reports.

One of the primary concerns in gathering information from people is whether the participants could be harmed in any way. The benefits of data collection should outweigh any potential harm, but to make this determination potential risks (physical, psychological, social, etc.) must be identified beforehand to the extent possible.

One way of reducing or preventing harm to subjects is the practice of keeping participation in data collection private. This is normally done by ensuring that participation is anonymous or confidential. Anonymity means not knowing which subjects provided which data, such as when individuals respond to a written questionnaire but do not include their names or other identifying information (e.g., social security number) on the question set. Once questionnaires like these are collected, there is no way to know which answers belong to whom, and so all responses are anonymous. Sometimes, however, anonymous responses are not possible. For instance, when an interview takes place in person, it is impossible for the interviewer not to know what an individual person said. In such a case, the interviewer is obliged to keep the identity of the respondent private, to maintain confidentiality. Although focus groups in Project CATE were both audiotaped and videotaped, when the transcriptions and analyses were done, the participants were referred to by gender, age, and a sequential number, never by name.

When people are the information source, it is also important that they consent voluntarily to give the information. Participants must understand why they are being asked to supply information, what their participation will entail (filling out a survey, being interviewed, etc.), and that they can choose not to participate. Generally speaking, when respondents are minors, a parent or legal guardian must provide informed consent, and the minor is asked to agree to participate. This process ensures that the young people themselves wish to participate and understand why their participation is important and what they are expected to do.

In most instances, it is a good idea to take the time with young participants to make sure they understand why the library's information gathering process is relevant to them. Many children have no experience in these matters and may not really understand what they are expected to do. When young participants understand the goals of information gathering and that they are helping the library serve youth better, they are better subjects. In addition, providing clear expectations about what participation means and using language appropriate to the developmental level of the participant are important not only for soliciting participation but for ensuring that the data collected are valid.

Surveys

A survey is a data collection method in which information is gathered through a questionnaire. The questionnaire may be self-administered, meaning respondents fill it out on their own, or an interviewer responsible for asking questions and recording respondent answers may administer it. Survey questionnaires can be administered through the mail, in person, by telephone, or by electronic means (Web, e-mail, instant messenger). The process of designing a survey involves developing a questionnaire (or obtaining an established questionnaire if one exists that meets the library's needs), determining a sampling strategy, administering the questionnaire, and analyzing the answers.

Surveys are one of the most popular forms of data collection used today. They are an excellent way to collect data from large samples and are especially good at measuring attitude, opinion, and knowledge. Surveys are also good because, when questionnaires are well formulated and administered, the potential for interviewer bias can be avoided.

Surveys are also popular because they are a relatively inexpensive way to collect data, they provide a means for collecting data quickly, and when self-administered they are a good method of eliciting candid responses, especially when the topic is somewhat sensitive. The keys to using this method of data collection are a good questionnaire and good sample selection.

DEVELOPING THE QUESTIONNAIRE

To develop an effective questionnaire, it is important to know what information the survey is designed to gather and who is likely to have the needed information. It is always best to go to the person who has the answer firsthand to ensure the validity of the data. For example, it is best to ask teachers questions that pertain to them as teachers—their own attitudes, observations, and knowledge—and not to ask them what they think parents, principals, or students think or want. Sometimes this kind of indirect questioning must be used because it is not possible to get access to the target group, but it is always better to get access to the people who have the information and let them speak for themselves.

To identify who has the needed information, consider who the stakeholders are. Stakeholders include the target user for your program or service as well as people inside and outside the library. Stakeholders in the library include librarians, administrators, and staff at all levels. Stakeholders outside the library may include funding agencies, competitors, non-users, parents, teachers, and various types of community leaders interested in youth. Additional stakeholders that may or may not be pertinent to planning include government bodies, library networks, library associations, and suppliers. In Project CATE the stakeholders who participated in data collection were parents (including some home-school parents), teachers, library staff (including administrators), and youth in grades four through eight (both users and non-users).

The best questionnaires ask questions that gather the needed information and are clearly worded and short. Although it seems straightforward to say that questions should make sense in terms of what the library wants to know, there is often a temptation to collect additional data, just because the library is going to exert this effort now. Sometimes there is a sense of wanting to be safe rather than sorry—and thus collecting data that just *might* be useful later—but it is a better strategy to limit information gathering to what is pertinent now. Avoiding irrelevant questions keeps the questionnaire as short as possible, which makes it less intimidating to respondents and easier to administer, code, and analyze.

The wording of questions is critical. Keep questions as short and simple as possible and clear enough that respondents can understand them easily. If the survey is to be used with young children, consider using graphics in place of text where possible. Be careful about including technical terms and jargon in the questions. This will be a special challenge when the questionnaire addresses technology. It is possible for people to make use of computers without knowing the technical names for the tools they are using, yet it is difficult to refer to technological things and procedures without using technical terms.

The solution to handling terms that describe technology and its use depend, in part, on who is responding to the questions. Technological terms, library terms, and other jargon are less a problem for some user groups than for others. In some cases, it is better to let respondents describe in their own words how they use technology or what kind of technological services they want the library to provide, or even what outcomes they are looking for in their technology or library use. Understanding the persons responding is critical to constructing questions they can answer.

When working with youth or with adult populations for whom literacy is a concern, it is important to consider the respondent reading level. If respondents cannot read independently, consider administering the survey rather than asking participants to fill it out. Surveys administered by library staff or trained representatives tend to get higher levels of participation than self-administered surveys; they also make it possible for individuals with low literacy skills to participate without feeling self-conscious about their lack of skill.

When collecting data from users who are not fluent in English or who may be more comfortable communicating in a language other than English, it is important to translate the questionnaire into the languages needed to facilitate information gathering. It is also important to have interviewers who speak the user's native language if the survey is to be administered. Translation and administration of a survey in the primary language of the users demonstrates the importance the library places on serving the community, improves community relations, and allows the library to be truly responsive to user needs.

CONSTRUCTING THE QUESTIONNAIRE

Generally, survey questions are of two types, open and closed. Open questions are those that ask people to respond to questions in their own words, such as this one:

> If you could choose any topic for a class presentation provided by the library, what would you most like to see? _____
>
> _____
> _____
> _____

Closed questions are those that provide or imply a fixed set of possible answers for the respondent. These can be questions that ask the respondent to choose between two choices, such as "yes" and "no." Or they can ask the respondent to choose from a list of possible answers. In this case, it is important that each item in the list be a distinct choice, with no overlap in the meanings of different items in the list. In addition, respondents can be offered the opportunity to provide an answer that does not fit the items provided or to expand on their answer, as in these two examples:

> Having the computers in the public library is important to me:
>
> a. Yes _____   b. No _____   c. Not sure _____
>
> Please tell us why you said yes or no or not sure: _____
> _____
> _____
>
> Besides the public library, I use computers at:
> *(Check every place you use a computer.)*
>
> a. home _____   e. parentís or caregiverís workplace _____
>
> b. school _____   f. store _____
>
> c. friendís house _____   g. community center _____
>
> d. relativeís house _____   h. where else? _____

Giving people the options of providing a different answer or more detail is an important practice that helps ensure respondents answer all questions with answers that reflect what they really think, feel, know, or do. When people are asked to choose a response that does not fit them or their situation, they are likely either to leave the question unanswered or to choose one of the options even though it is not really a "right" answer for them. When this happens, the validity of the data collected in the survey is at risk.

Another type of survey question is one that allows respondents to indicate their opinion on a scale, as shown here:

How important do you think it is to have someone available to help students use the computers in the public library?

Very important				*Not important at all*		
1	2	3	4	5	6	7

Ratings on a scale can be useful in a variety of ways. For example, they can be used to characterize level of support (agree, uncertain, disagree), frequency of an activity (never, occasionally, frequently), rating of performance (poor, good, excellent), or comparisons (worse, same, better).

One of the best ways to ensure that the questionnaire does its job is to pretest it before using it to collect data. This saves both time and expense by revealing problems with the survey while there is still an opportunity to improve it. To pretest the questionnaire, ask users who are similar to those who will be asked to participate in the study to fill it out, or let someone from the library administer it to them, to determine if the questions are understood as intended. Then talk to those who did the pretest to understand how they perceived the questions. If the pretest reveals that the questions need reworking to improve clarity or ensure that they gather the type of information needed, this is a sign that the questionnaire is not ready for use. Refine it and pretest again until the questionnaire is easy to administer and readily understood by pretest respondents. A sample survey used to evaluate Club Tech for Project CATE is provided in appendix A.

FINDING AND RECRUITING PARTICIPANTS

One of the strengths of surveys is that, with a well-chosen sample, it is possible to generalize findings to a defined population. The first step in deciding who to ask to respond to the questionnaire is to identify all members of the population. Examples of defined populations include preschool age children who live in the library's service area, youth in grades four through six who attend local schools, and youth ages twelve to eighteen who live in the library's service area.

In most cases it is not reasonable to expect to survey every person in the population. Unless the population is very small, the effort and cost of such an

BROWN BAG DELI-WESTHEI
2036 WESTHEIMER STE D
HOUSTON, TX 77098

TERMINAL ID: 006393458
MERCHANT #:   469165106888

MC
#xxxxxxxxxxxxx1015
SUR: 1
SALE
BATCH: 000225   INVOICE: 025967
DATE: NOV 15, 07   TIME: 11:43
SQ: 011   AUTH NO: 082080

                        $9.74
PRE-TIP AMT

TIP   ------------

TOTAL   ------------

CUSTOMER COPY

...eat. For this reason, it is more common to select ...on, a sample, to complete the questionnaire. The ...rtant to generalize what is learned from the sam-...lation they represent, is to draw a random sam-...ns that every member of the population defined ...nce of being selected to participate in the study. ...st the possibility of a biased sample by ensuring ...ion is chance.

...n Level I and Level II projects it may not make ...d to ensure that a random sample is achieved. ...ndom sampling are discussed below. For Level III pro..., however, the selection of a random sample helps ensure that planning and evaluation decisions are based on information that represents the user group.

Selecting a random sample. The first step in selecting a random sample is to identify or construct a sampling frame, which is a list that identifies every member of the population of interest. For example, if the population of interest is third-grade students attending public school in the designated service area, school registration records could serve as the sampling frame. A random sample of third graders attending public school in the library's service area could be drawn from this list.

In most instances, it is easier to use an existing list as the sampling frame than to construct one. Whether an existing list is used or one is constructed, care must be taken to make sure that it is complete and accurate. For an example like the one mentioned above, remember that children leave and enter schools throughout the year; it is important to make sure that the sampling frame is current.

When names are selected from the sampling frame, a random selection process must be used. A common method of random selection is pulling names out of a hat. A better way is to number all the entries on the list, generate random numbers, and then select those numbers on your list that match the random numbers generated. There are random number tables designed for this purpose as well as computer programs that generate random numbers. Instructions on using a random number table can be found in Babbie (2004) and Powell and Connaway (2004).

Another way to draw a random sample is to determine how large the sample will be, divide this number by the number of people in the population, and then, after finding a random place in the list to start, choose every *n*th entry. This is called systematic random sampling. For example, if the sampling frame consists of 2,000 names and a sample of 200 people is needed, every tenth person on the list can be chosen to be a respondent in the survey. Be sure, though, to start at a random place in the list. This procedure can be as simple as pulling a number out of a hat. That number pulled determines the first name selected, and from there every tenth person is chosen to participate in the study until 200 names are identified.

Sometimes it is important to make sure that certain characteristics in the sample are equally represented, depending on the information needed. For instance, if the library is interested in gender differences in computer use, it is important that the sample include similar numbers of boys and girls. Stratified random sampling is the process used for this purpose. For instance, in response to the example above, the sampling frame would be rearranged so that boys and girls are separated into different groupings. It would then be possible to take a random sample of girls and a random sample of boys to be respondents in the study.

Alternatives to random sampling. It is always preferable to use random sampling strategies but not always possible to do so. Sampling frames do not exist for every population of interest to libraries. When it is not possible to obtain or create a list of all members of a population, such as non-users, it may be necessary to use a non-probability (non-random) sampling approach. There are limitations to the types of analysis that can be performed on data collected by non-probability sampling, and the findings of studies that use such sampling cannot be used to generalize about the population the sample is meant to reflect. For instance, a survey of non-users selected by a non-probability method would describe what the non-users who participated in the study think, know, or do, but it would not necessarily describe the opinions, knowledge, or behavior of all non-users in the service area.

The main concern when selecting participants is always that the resulting sample comprise individuals who have the information needed and who are representative of the population of interest. Non-probability approaches include recruiting subjects because they are easily accessible, choosing subjects based on an understanding of the target population, and identifying members of the target population and asking them to identify other respondents for study.

Calculating sample size. Defining the population and deciding what kind of sample is needed are both prerequisites to determining how many respondents are needed for data collection. In general, the larger a sample is, the more representative of the population it is likely to be. At the same time, it does not make sense to collect more data than are needed in terms of cost and effort.

Some factors that affect sample size are the level of variability in the population (how alike or unalike the individuals in the population are), how many variables are being studied, whether subgroups of the population are to be compared, the kind of statistics to be used to analyze the data, and how precise the relationship between the sample and the population needs to be.

As a rule of thumb, some writers suggest that a minimum of 100 respondents is necessary to achieve a representative sample of a population when performing a typical library service evaluation (Powell and Connaway 2004; Walter 1992). In Project CATE, minimum samples of 100 were sought for parents, teachers, community leaders, and students.

One approach to determining sample size is to use a sample size table developed for this purpose, such as the one provided in table 7-1. Sample size tables assign sample sizes on the basis of population size. To use this table, locate the size of the population (column *N*), and the sample size needed for that population is given in column *S*. For example, if the number of preschool children in the library's service area is 15,000, the suggested sample size is 375.

The most accurate way to determine sample size is to use statistical formulas developed for this purpose. If the process of determining a sample seems overwhelming, remember that help is available. State library agencies, local universities, library associations, library consultants, and other libraries are all possible avenues for finding assistance when you have questions about the information gathering process.

Response rate and optimizing participation. The response rate is a measure of the degree of participation in a survey. If 200 questionnaires are sent out in the mail, for example, it is unlikely that all of these will be filled out and returned to the library. If 100 of the 200 mailings are returned, the response rate is 50 percent. Poor response rate not only limits the types of statistical tests that can be used in data analysis, it can also turn a well-planned probability sample into a non-probability sample. A return rate of less than 50 percent suggests that the data collected are not representative of the population (Babbie 2004).

There are several ways to increase participation in a survey. The first consideration is the design of the questionnaire itself—how it is laid out, the typeface and white space allowed, and the length. The goal is a questionnaire that does not look like it will take a huge effort to complete. Be sure to provide the questionnaire in respondents' preferred language if languages other than English are used by the target population.

If the questionnaire will be self-administered through the mail, make it as easy as possible for respondents to complete and return it to the library. Include

Table 7-1

Table for Determining Sample Size for a Given Population

N	S	N	S	N	S
10	10	220	140	1200	291
15	14	230	144	1300	297
20	19	240	148	1400	302
25	24	250	152	1500	306
30	28	260	155	1600	310
35	32	270	159	1700	313
40	36	280	162	1800	317
45	40	290	165	1900	320
50	44	300	169	2000	322
55	48	320	175	2200	327
60	52	340	181	2400	331
65	56	360	186	2600	335
70	59	380	191	2800	338
75	63	400	196	3000	341
80	66	420	201	3500	346
85	70	440	205	4000	351
90	73	460	210	4500	354
95	76	480	214	5000	357
100	80	500	217	6000	361
110	86	550	226	7000	364
120	92	600	234	8000	367
130	97	650	242	9000	368
140	103	700	248	10000	370
150	108	750	254	15000	375
160	113	800	260	20000	377
170	118	850	265	30000	379
180	123	900	269	40000	380
190	127	950	274	50000	381
200	132	1000	278	75000	382
210	136	1100	285	100000	384

N is population size. *S* is sample size. From Krejcie and Morgan (1970, 608). Reprinted with permission of Sage Publications.

a stamped, self-addressed envelope or other mechanism to make it easy for respondents to send the completed survey back. Consider offering to pick up completed surveys. Monitor the number of surveys returned, and send follow-up notes or telephone to remind respondents that their participation is important. Consider administering the surveys in person if possible. Questionnaires administered in person typically have better return rates than mail surveys do.

Other ways to increase participation include providing an incentive to participants, such as giving token gifts or offering drawings for a prize. Another way to increase participation is to collaborate with local organizations that are also interested in the target population. These organizations can assist by encouraging participation among their members.

DATA ANALYSIS

The right time to think about how data will be analyzed is during the development of the questionnaire. If the project is a Level III effort, it is likely that the data collection and analysis will be extensive and may require the assistance of statistical software programs or a professional consultant. If the data is for a Level I or Level II project and only a limited amount is to be collected, analysis without outside help or special tools may be possible.

Because surveys tend to be descriptive, it is normally possible to assign numeric values to answers and to calculate frequencies and response rates that summarize the data. If the survey contains a question about grade, for example, the number of respondents at each grade level can be summed and then described as a percentage of the total respondents; if there are 400 respondents, the percentage and number that respond in each grade category might be reported as "12.5 percent (50) respondents in grade four," "12.5 percent (50) respondents in grade five," "25 percent (100) respondents in grade six," "25 percent (100) respondents in grade seven," and "25 percent (100) respondents in grade eight." Because most of the work of setting categories is done in the development of closed questions, they can be entered directly into statistical and spreadsheet software with minimal preparation, and frequencies and response rates are easily calculated. Again, when data collection is limited, it may be possible to perform these operations without the assistance of software.

Open-ended questions require more effort, since answers must be analyzed and placed into categories before the data can be summarized and quantified. The first step in looking at responses to open-ended questions is to sort the data into mutually exclusive categories. Because respondents use their own words in open-ended questions, they may use different words to say the same thing. A question about computer use in the library, for example, might elicit the responses "e-mail," "communicate with friends and family," "chat rooms," "play games," and "do homework." The first three responses could be labeled as communication use, "play games" as recreational use, and "do homework" as imposed use. The categories used will depend on the intent of the question and the type of responses received. Once the data are placed in categories, they can then be entered into software for summarization and quantification.

Although it is possible to do this kind of quantification by hand, if there are many questionnaires the use of statistical or spreadsheet software makes the job more efficient by organizing the data, limiting calculation errors, and keeping the data in a form that makes multiple calculations faster and easier. Using software also has the advantage of making it easy to produce graphs and charts that can be exported to word processing software and used in reports and presentations. Examples of typical software for this purpose include SPSS and Microsoft Excel.

Focus Groups and In-Depth Interviews

Along with large-scale surveys, focus groups and in-depth interviews can be used to gather information from people to improve or inform the development and delivery of library programs and services. Focus groups are discussions moderated by a leader and typically involve seven to fifteen people. In-depth interviews involve two people, an interviewer and a respondent.

Focus groups and in-depth interviews can be more or less structured, depending on the intent of the question set. In structured focus groups and in-depth interviews, the goal is to collect responses to a set of predetermined questions, similar to administering a survey but allowing for discussion. An unstructured question guide is developed when the intent is to explore a topic area in depth. In this case, the concern is not to gather responses to preformulated questions but rather to let the participants take the conversation where they wish to express their experience, opinions, and concerns.

In planning focus groups, it is important to decide ahead of time whether they will be structured or unstructured. Structured focus groups can involve more participants, since the general discussion is directed and controlled more overtly by the moderator. In an unstructured focus group, the moderator spends more time probing for detail, so smaller groups allow more time for individual respondents to express themselves. In Project CATE the questions were structured, although not rigidly followed.

It is preferable that participants selected for focus groups not know each other but be similar in relevant respects. For instance, it is better to have separate focus groups for staff members and for users rather than a single group that combines the two. When young people are participants in focus groups, group membership should be limited to no more than a two-year age or grade span, and groups separated by gender are also a good idea (Siegel, Coffey, and Livingston 2001; Zollo 1999). In Project CATE focus groups, the two-year range was adhered to except in a single group that included nine- to thirteen-year-olds; the latter was the least successful of the groups.

The typical focus group runs about 90 minutes; however, with youth, depending on age, this may be too long. Walter (1992) suggests that with children a 30- to 45-minute focus group is normal. Staff for focus groups include a moderator and note taker. In addition, it is useful to record group sessions to ensure that all data are available for analysis. A videotaped session, when practical, ensures the preservation of much of the data, including body language and expression. If this is not possible, be sure to audiotape the session. In-depth interviews should be audiotaped too. Whenever recording devices are to be used, be sure to test them ahead of time.

It is important to set the tone for a focus group or in-depth interview as a comfortable place for the exchange of ideas. The moderator should introduce him/herself and any other staff members in the room, then explain why the focus group is being held, how the process will work, and what is expected from the participants. Participants should know if the session is being recorded and that their participation will be kept confidential. Start the session with some warm-up questions. Let everyone in the room introduce him/herself. Provide participants with nametags or name tents that identify first names only. It helps the transcription process for the moderator to mention names when interacting with participants. It is good to have someone taking notes and identifying each speaker in turn if videotaping is not possible, because moderators may forget to call each speaker by name, and some responses are spontaneous rather than solicited.

Participants should do the talking, and usually one of the goals is to encourage interaction between group members. It is the moderator's job to keep the discussion going, to bring out those who are quiet, and to keep stronger personalities from dominating the discussion. The moderator may wish to make notes during the discussion of important points but should not be the only note taker in the room. One or more designated note takers should keep track of as much of the total conversation as possible. In Project CATE, library staff members did all the data collection. One member moderated, usually a librarian, and another took notes. Neither moderator nor note takers should offer their opinions concerning any of the focus group questions. At the end of the session, the recorders are turned off and the moderator thanks the participants and reminds them again of the importance of their responses for improving library service.

Focus groups and in-depth interviews have many uses. They are excellent ways to understand the experiences, opinions, and attitudes of individuals and to see the library from the participants' points of view. These approaches are useful for gathering data that will inform the development of a survey questionnaire. They are also useful methods after a survey study to reach a deeper understanding of survey questionnaire responses and to probe any questions that come up in the analysis of the survey data. It is important to remember that, although focus groups and in-depth interviews are useful ways to collect data, they are not generalizable. This means that it is not a good idea to base decisions on this kind of data alone, but rather to use it to complement other data sources.

DEVELOPING THE INTERVIEW GUIDE

The interview guide provides a framework for the discussion in either a focus group or an in-depth interview. It outlines the questions and probes meant to encourage participants to elaborate on the topic. Construct open-ended interview guide questions to elicit as much discussion as possible. Begin the interview guide with general, nonthreatening questions to allow participants to warm up and feel comfortable. Try to order the questions in a logical sequence.

Remember that in unstructured focus groups and in in-depth interviews, the interview guide is a framework, not a rigid schedule. In these situations the discussion should be allowed to unfold naturally and follow the lead of the respondents. The interview guide provides a place to begin the conversation, but the moderator should allow the conversation to deviate from the guide as necessary, staying within the subject range of interest to the investigation. Interview guides, like survey questionnaires, should be pretested with members of the target audience who will not be participating in the study. Pretesting ensures that the questions are written at the right level for the target group, are easy to understand, and will elicit the needed information. Sample focus group questions used in Project CATE are provided in appendix A.

FINDING AND RECRUITING PARTICIPANTS

Participants in focus groups and in-depth interviews are representative of the target population. If, for instance, the focus group or in-depth interview is interested in the opinions of middle school girls, middle school girls will be sought for participation. Finding participants can, however, be a challenge. Potential sources of young participants include advertisements in school newspapers, local parent/teacher organizations, Friends of the Library, library users, and local children's organizations. The literature (Bertot, McClure, and Ryan 2000; Walter 1992; Zollo 1999) suggests, as a rule, that four groups is often sufficient for typical library data gathering to obtain the information sought, but also that there is no point in continuing focus groups if no new data are being revealed.

Recruiting sufficient participation in focus groups can be surprisingly hard, so it is common practice to pay for participation, and refreshments should always be offered at a focus group meeting. Compensation for participation can take the form of a cash payment, a gift certificate, or some other kind of gift. Zollo (1999) suggests over-recruiting for focus groups as one way to make sure there are a sufficient number of participants. The children and adults in Project CATE were paid $20 for taking part in a focus group. Remember that, even though fifteen people may have agreed to participate in a focus group, not all of them will show up. Collaborating with local organizations interested in your target group is another way to solicit participation for focus groups and in-depth interviews.

DATA ANALYSIS

Typically, focus group and interview data are analyzed by reviewing transcripts, notes, and any other documentation recorded to discover themes and patterns in the participants' remarks. In contrast to the analysis of survey data, focus group and in-depth interview data analysis should begin as soon as the first interview or focus group takes place—because what is learned from each focus group or interview will be used to shape the questions asked or issues probed in the next focus group or interview. As information is gathered, analyzed, and gathered again, important themes and patterns begin to emerge and clarify. When data collection reaches a point where no new understandings emerge, but only reinforcements of earlier findings, it is time for data collection to stop.

Much has been written on performing various types of content analysis. One of the best written for use in library research is *Naturalistic Inquiry for Library Science: Methods and Applications for Research, Evaluation, and Teaching* (Mellon 1990). Other useful texts include Glaser and Strauss (1967), Miles and Huberman (1994), and Weber (1990). There are also computer programs that can be used for qualitative analysis. QSR NUD*IST was used in Project CATE to pull themes from the focus groups and to reveal relationships between these themes and factors of interest such as gender and age.

Observation

Observation is perhaps the oldest method used to study youth (McNeal 1999). It is used in both laboratory studies and studies of behavior in "natural" environments such as schools and libraries. In strict, unobtrusive, observational studies, it is important to observe without interacting in the environment and to use strategies to ensure that the subjects are unaware that they are being studied. The point of this type of research is to see what the observed subjects do naturally, and often when people know that they are being observed they change their behavior.

Observation can take many forms. Unobtrusive observation can mean sitting at a table in the children's room and watching the action, or it can mean using electronic tools such as log analysis to observe what users are doing at the computers. In both cases, the key similarity is that the observer is only observing and not performing any action that might influence what the subjects of the observation do.

In another form of observation, participant observation, the observer does interact with subjects, and the participants know that the observer is watching them and why. This type of observation is dependent on the relationship between the observer and the subjects and the willingness of participants to be candid. In-depth interviewing, described above, is one form of participant observation.

Like focus groups, observational research may be structured or unstructured. The strength of observation is that it is an excellent measure of what people actually do, which may be different from what people say they do. For example, in Project CATE focus group interviews, children reported gender differences in computer use that were not reflected in systematic observations in the library or in survey data. Such differences between perceptions of use and actual behavior are important for the development of programs and services.

Using observation to gather information also has limitations. It is, for instance, a weak method of determining why subjects behave in a certain way, how subjects see the situation they are in, or how they feel about the situation or environment. If information concerning attitudes, perceptions, motivations, or opinions is needed, surveys or in-depth interviews are better choices for data collection.

PLANNING AN OBSERVATION

The first steps in planning an observation are to decide who will be observed, what will be observed, where the observation will take place, and when. These decisions must make sense in terms of the information sought. In Project CATE young people from grades four through eight were the population of interest, and the focus was on understanding their use of computers in the library. It was important to the study to collect baseline data on how these young people used computers, both to inform program and service development and to provide a basis for comparison for future evaluations.

In this instance, then, the "who" to be observed were youth in the target grade range and the "where" was at the library computers. In a structured observation, the "what" to be observed must be carefully thought through before the observation takes place. This process is similar in some ways to the development of a survey questionnaire in that the categories for observation are identified ahead of time, although it is still possible to record additional relevant observations as they appear.

The central concern of the Project CATE observation was the content of the computer screen at the time the observation took place. But to respond fully to the requirements of the research project, ancillary data such as user age, grade, and gender were recorded, as well as contextual data such as computer type (e.g., at the computer catalog, or a computer that required an appointment). In addition, the date, time, branch where the observation took place, and name of the person performing the observation were recorded to allow for analysis by branch and time and to provide a contact in case questions arose concerning a particular observation. Library staff members were trained in use of the PDAs and in observational skills to collect this data. The observation guide for Project CATE is provided in appendix A.

The question of "when" to observe can be approached in a variety of ways. Observations might be performed at random times throughout the day. Project CATE adopted the standard approach used in the output measurement literature (Bertot, McClure, and Ryan 2000; Walter 1992, 1995), which recommends collecting data during a representative week or weeks in the library and then extrapolating counts to estimate annual use. The key to this process is that the data collection week must be representative of normal library use. This means that weeks in which holidays, special closings, other local events, as well as those during which there is severe weather, should be avoided, since these events may affect library use. Walter (1992, 1995) also points out that the local school schedule can influence library use and thus should be considered. In districts with year-round schools, one full week of data collection may be sufficient. In districts that follow the traditional school schedule, two weeks of data collection are necessary, since a typical week in summer is different from a typical week during the school year.

DATA ANALYSIS

In a structured observation where the categories of observation are determined ahead of time, quantitative analysis is typical. In an unstructured observation, categories must be developed on the basis of the observed behaviors and may be treated either quantitatively or qualitatively, depending on what the research is designed to find out. The data analysis methods described under survey research and focus groups above are also appropriate for use with data collected through observation.

■   ■   ■

The collection and analysis of information, reviewed in this chapter and chapter 6, lead to the development of desired outcomes, to which we now turn in chapter 8, to approaches to refining programs and services (chapter 9), and to evaluations of the degree to which programs and services achieve their outcomes (chapter 10).

Eight

Phase II

Determining Outcomes

Phase II of the CATE OBPE model uses the information gathered in Phase I as a basis for choosing outcomes the library wants in developing programs and services. To decide which outcomes to pursue, it is necessary to know

- what program or service area is being developed
- how this development fits into the library's strategic plan

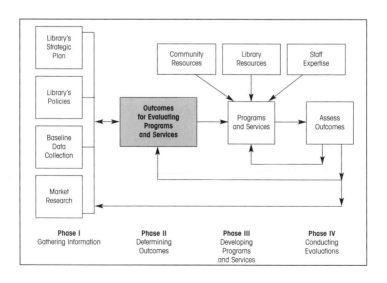

Phase I	Phase II	Phase III	Phase IV
Gathering Information	Determining Outcomes	Developing Programs and Services	Conducting Evaluations

- the level of the effort planned (as described in chapter 4)
- who the target audience (user) is
- what the user and other stakeholders have to say about desired outcomes for this program or service area

If any of this information is missing or not current, this is a signal that the information gathering of Phase I is incomplete and that more information must be gathered.

Considering Potential Outcomes

The goal of Phase II is to determine what benefits or impacts users, other stakeholders, and the library want users to experience in the identified library program or service area. These potential outcomes relate to changes in knowledge, skill, behavior, attitude, or status. A change in knowledge, for example, might relate to increasing the number of Internet sites a student knows about that are helpful for homework and a change in skill level might mean improving preliteracy skills among young children. An example of a change in behavior is helping young people use digital resources independently. A change in attitude might mean giving young people the experience of reading as fun, and a change in status might be helping people bridge the divide between not knowing how to use computers and becoming computer users.

Deciding which outcomes to pursue in a given program or service area requires an analysis of the library's strategic plan and the opinions of the intended users and other interested stakeholders. Gathering these opinions may have been part of strategic planning or may require additional data collection during Phase I. Surveys, interviews, and focus groups, as discussed in chapter 7, are all effective methods of gathering opinions from users, staff, and other stakeholders. This information is then analyzed and summarized to determine

- the extent of agreement among the interested parties
- the extent to which desired outcomes make sense in terms of the library's mission, goals, and objectives
- the capacity of desired outcomes to maximize the library's identified strengths and opportunities

Choosing outcomes is easiest when the results of this analysis reveal a consensus among stakeholders that is also a good match with the library's established goals and objectives. In cases where there is not a strongly shared desire for a specific outcome, the library may want to choose the outcome or outcomes most closely aligned with established library goals and objectives, understanding that choice of outcome to pursue will be assessed again in the future. It is also possible, in cases where there is little consensus, to decide to address a broad array of outcomes in the development of programs and services. If users and stakeholders desire outcomes from library use that are outside library goals and objectives, this signals a need to rethink the library's mission and service roles, since these may no longer reflect community needs.

The process of choosing and defining desired outcomes as part of planning and before program and service development starts is an important feature of the CATE OBPE model. In the absence of this kind of planning, outcome measurement is in danger of becoming a process of "fishing" for outcomes rather than the kind of deliberate, user-responsive process the CATE OBPE model advocates. Although fishing for outcomes may reveal impacts and benefits experienced by library users, it is unlikely to help the library maximize user benefits or provide benefits that speak to the core interests of users and stakeholders in a proactive manner. Unanticipated outcomes can be incorporated in ongoing planning if deemed appropriate, but they must not be used to replace OBPE. Fishing for outcomes may provide some interesting data, but it is unlikely to provide the kind of process that strengthens the library's ability to plan for and achieve its goals.

In Project CATE, the data collected in Phase I expressed interest among stakeholders in a variety of outcomes, but there was a clear emphasis in each stakeholder group on the need for increased computer knowledge and skills among the target audience. In terms of knowledge, the concerns were increasing the number of good websites young people are aware of, increasing knowledge of safety issues, and increasing awareness of intellectual property issues in the use of electronic information resources. Stakeholders were interested in a wide variety of computer skills, including basic keyboarding and computer skills, searching skills, software application use, and the ability to troubleshoot hardware problems and create websites.

The level of the effort planned is also a consideration when determining which outcomes to pursue in developing programs and services. There is no magic number of outcomes needed, but choosing to embrace multiple outcomes may not make sense for Level I programs, which are either one-time offerings or stand-alone programs designed to fit a specific purpose. In such cases, one or at most two outcomes are likely to be all that can be accomplished by a single program or service.

A single outcome can also be a sufficient goal for a Level II or even Level III program or service. It is not unusual for a desired outcome to have several dimensions that may require multiple programs for achieving the full range of desired skills, knowledge, behavior, attitude, or status change. Further, if analysis shows that stakeholders are concerned with only one or two types of outcomes, it does not make sense to try to achieve other additional outcomes.

In cases where stakeholders demonstrate emphasis on multiple outcomes and the library sees this as viable in the context of the strategic plan, program and service development must be coordinated and may comprise a variety of approaches, including program development at all three levels of effort during the planning cycle.

As mentioned in chapters 2, 3, and 5, the types of outcomes identified by the United Way provide a useful framework for thinking about how programs and services can benefit users. Planning for outcomes does, however, also have the potential to effect change beyond the immediate impact on users. The benefits of outcome-based planning can occur at the user level, the library level, the community level, the professional practice level, and beyond, and it is possible to plan for specific desired outcomes at each level of the library's influence. For instance, the development of "best practice" in a service area can affect professional practice (behavior) at the system, state, or national level.

Outcomes also have a time dimension. Effective programs and services have outcomes that can provide immediate benefits to those who engage in library programs and services. These immediate benefits can also accrue over time, resulting in future benefits at the individual level and, potentially, in the community, library, and the profession at large. For example, the short-term benefits of increased technological skill may help students do a better job of using computers to complete homework assignments. Over time this increase in skill may assist students to perform better in school overall and later may affect statistics such as number of students who enter college or engage in other types of post–high school education. In the long term, this may lead to more young people better prepared to compete in the job market. Effective library programs strengthen the profession of librarianship and the role of libraries in communities, and they further the funding and development of additional library programs and services.

The CATE OBPE model is most directly concerned with outcomes at the individual level and in the short term but, even with a focus on the individual level, it can benefit the organization that participates in this process and the community as a whole. At the St. Louis Public Library the organizational culture and staff orientation, which were already user focused, became more attentive to the connection between program and service provision and the potential to benefit individuals. The process of evaluation became more pertinent as it became clear that evaluation was more than numbers on reports; evaluation provided live feedback that staff members could use to assess their own performance and improve their ability to achieve desired outcomes with users. This example highlights the potential for unanticipated outcomes that may be experienced by the target population, other stakeholders, the library, the community, and the profession of librarianship. Keep in mind that, even when programs and services are tailored to provide certain outcomes, it is not uncommon for multiple benefits to follow from these efforts.

Defining Desired Outcomes

Once the outcomes to be pursued in program or service development have been selected, the next steps are to

- develop a description of the desired outcomes
- determine how the library will know when an outcome has been achieved
- determine how to measure outcomes

These steps are central to the design of programs and services, evaluation, and the ability to describe the benefits and impacts users received from their library use. Completing these steps is the key to answering the question, How will you know if programs and services are achieving the desired outcomes for users?

Describing Outcomes

To achieve a specific outcome, it is important to be able to describe it. When a program or service is designed and developed to provide an outcome that is specific, it is likely to be more effective in achieving it. A clear statement of the desired outcome makes it easier to communicate the intended benefits of a program and service to staff, users, and other stakeholders in the life of the library. Similarly, a higher level of detail in an outcome description simplifies program and service development and makes it possible to tailor approaches to user needs.

First and foremost, it is important to know what type of change or impact the desired outcome represents. Is it a change in knowledge, skill, behavior, attitude, or status? This initial step is critical for communicating the objectives and results of program and service development and for gaining common understanding among all stakeholders. Once the outcome type is established, the next step is to develop a one-sentence description that expresses what the outcome is to achieve. For example, a typical behavior outcome description might be "increased independent use of digital resources," and a typical skill outcome description might be "ability to use the library catalog."

Once the type of outcome and a brief outcome description are settled, it is possible to continue to refine the description by providing more detail about what the desired outcome "looks like." Think about how it is possible to tell if a particular behavior, attitude, or skill has been achieved. In the skill example above, ability to use the library catalog is not best assessed with a "yes or no" question. The ability to use the library catalog is more complicated than that. A better way to think about users' ability to use the catalog is to categorize library catalog skills as basic, intermediate, and advanced. The basic level might comprise general skills needed to do a search for a known item. A person with intermediate skills might be expected to have these basic skills but also to know how to perform a subject search. At the advanced level, a user would have both basic and intermediate skills but could also take advantage of features that allow more user control over searches and change the way records are displayed.

Table 8-1 displays these three skill levels as described in Project CATE and used to describe, identify, and assess user ability. Note that each skill level builds on the one beneath it, and each level represents the attainment of more complex skills.

Skill descriptions such as these can function as guidelines that allow staff to assess competency levels quickly when interacting with users one-on-one or as part of a program or service. The descriptions also identify potential goals for the next logical step in helping users develop missing behaviors or skills they need to attain a level completely or to begin to learn a new one. It is possible to construct outcome-based criteria indicator tables for all of the outcome types and at varying levels of detail. The specification of outcomes at this level of detail allows a staff to target programs and services to specific tangible aims that can be discussed, aimed for, and measured.

Knowing When an Outcome Is Achieved

Specific definitions for desired outcomes indicate what an outcome looks like but not how to assess if an outcome has been achieved. The outcome-based criteria table also indicates what an outcome looks like but does indicate the skill level of an individual user or whether a program designed to improve user catalog skills is effective. What is needed is an indicator that demonstrates the presence of the outcome and the level at which it has been achieved.

Table 8-1
CATE OPBE, Phase II: Outcome-Based Criteria Table

Desired Outcome Type: Skill		
Description: Ability to Use the St. Louis Public Library Catalog		
Basic	**Intermediate**	**Advanced**
Understands what the library catalog is.	*Has achieved all the skills at Level I plus:*	*Has achieved all the skills at Levels I and II plus:*
Can recognize and access the catalog at a dedicated terminal in the library.	Can access the library catalog via the Web.	Can differentiate key words from assigned subject headings.
Understands basic bibliographic concepts, including author, title, subject, word versus phrase, search, and catalog.	Understands what a subject heading is.	Can determine when to use key words in which fields for the most efficient search strategy.
Can navigate the basic window search.	Can construct a subject search in the basic search mode.	Can limit search by language.
Can construct a basic search for an author or title.	Can recognize relevant subject headings in a list.	Can search by material type.
Can troubleshoot basic search problems such as spelling errors.	Can read and understand the full bibliographic record.	Can re-sort output lists as needed.
Can interpret the hit list.	Can use the subject headings associated with a relevant item to expand subject search.	Can place a request for items that are currently unavailable.
Can start a new search as needed.		Can apply the concepts from the library catalog to search behavior in other electronic catalogs and databases.
Can locate desired item in a response list.		
Can use citation and holdings record to locate item in the library.		

It is possible that more than one indicator will provide evidence that an outcome has been achieved. It may be possible to assess a user's skill with the library catalog through observation, by talking to him or her about the catalog, or by administering a test. In some cases, more than one indicator is needed to measure all the dimensions of an outcome. A change in attitude toward reading, for example, may be demonstrated by increased in-library use or check-out of library materials, better grades, increased satisfaction with the school experience, and increased self-identification as a "reader."

When considering which indicators to adopt to measure the presence of outcomes, some things to consider are the relative ease of using a particular indicator, which indicators provide the most valid data, and which indicators provide the best picture of the impact or benefits experienced by the user.

Measuring Outcomes

Indicators describe what to look for in assessing outcomes, but to assess and improve programs and services, indicators must be measured in a way that allows recording and reporting of the extent to which outcomes are achieved. Whatever method is used to measure outcomes, the primary considerations are that the method do a good job of measuring the indicator and that an appropriate data source be used. The methods discussed in chapter 7 are appropriate for use in measuring outcomes.

In the previous example of catalog skills, there are several ways to assess skill level and changes in skill level that result from library programs and services. The most obvious method of assessing skills is to test them. In this case, a test score is the measure of the user's ability. When a test is well constructed, it can be a good measure of skills or knowledge and provide an objective comparison of individuals' performances. Tests also provide a method for measuring the impact of a program. For instance, if the objective is to improve skill level, tests can indicate the skill levels of program participants before the program starts and then again after the program.

It is also possible to observe behavior as a way of assessing skill levels. When observation is used, the outcome-based criteria table can provide the structure for assessing performance. In St. Louis there was a strong library staff perception that the community was adverse to the idea of being tested, so strict skill tests were difficult to implement. However, when program activities result in products, the products themselves may provide a method of understanding a user's skill level at the end of the program. For instance, if as part of a lesson on using an application such as PowerPoint participants create their own presentations, not only is their process observable, but the quality of their presentation is also a measure of skills acquired in the lesson.

Other outcome types, such as attitude, are best measured with surveys and in-depth interviews, since these methods are particularly strong in measuring attitude and opinion. Changes in behavior can also be measured in surveys or interviews but are best measured by unobtrusive observation, because self-reports of behavior do not always reflect what people actually do. Methods best used to measure a change in status depend on how the specific change is defined and could include any of the methods described in chapter 7.

Stating Program and Service Objectives

The third task in developing outcome-based criteria to guide program and service development and evaluation is to set objectives to be achieved by the program or service during a defined time period. In addition to defining the timeframe for reaching these objectives, the objectives must be measurable, such as the percentage or number of participants who experience the desired outcome. Measurable performance objectives for the catalog skills might read something like this: "80 percent of youth grades six to ten who participate in a searching skills class will be able to use the catalog at the basic level at the end of the training session. 20 percent of youth grades six to ten who participate in a searching skills class will be able to use the catalog at the intermediate or advanced level at the end of the training session." Notice that the target user group is identified, the performance goal is measurable, and a timeframe is given within which the goal is to be achieved.

The main reason for developing performance objectives for programs and services is to be able to assess progress toward the attainment of desired outcomes and to share this progress with interested parties such as staff, stakeholders, the community, and funding agencies. Performance objectives also help improve library programs and services and guide decisions about which programs to offer and which to discontinue on the basis of their effectiveness.

Determining performance objectives should involve library staff and management and must be realistic in terms of the level of commitment, resources, and support invested in producing the programs and services. It is important for staff members to not only agree on the expectations for performance but also feel that the expectations are achievable.

Several inputs to determine performance objectives can help the library identify realistic program or service goals. Baseline data collected in Phase I are useful in determining objectives for performance, for they suggest what current performance looks like. Staff members may then consider how comfortable they are with that level of performance; they may want to set the bar higher. It is also possible to involve users and other stakeholders in the development of performance objectives. User expectations for library performance may offer a point of view that generates additional discussion.

When an outside agency is funding the program or service development, agency expectations are also a factor to consider. Is the funding agency imposing targets for performance the library must achieve? Is the attainment of future funding dependent on the library's ability to demonstrate a certain level of success? Increasingly, funding agencies are looking for outcome-based evaluations for the projects they support. Use of the CATE OBPE model is one way of demonstrating that the library is oriented toward and has the expertise necessary for providing a funding agency with outcome-based assessments.

■   ■   ■

The stage is now set in the CATE OBPE process for the development of programs and services in Phase III. The completion of Phase II has established the outcomes to be sought through program and service development and which indicators can be used as a basis for evaluating the extent to which programs and services are successful in achieving desired outcomes.

Nine

Phase III

Developing Programs and Services

Providing high-quality programming and direct service to individual children and young adults is at the heart of what youth services staffs do. Therefore, Phase III of the CATE OBPE model is likely to build on activities that are comfortable for youth services librarians and staff. But OBPE adds a set of guidelines and direction that may be new to many. In this chapter we address how to manage programs and services using the CATE OBPE model.

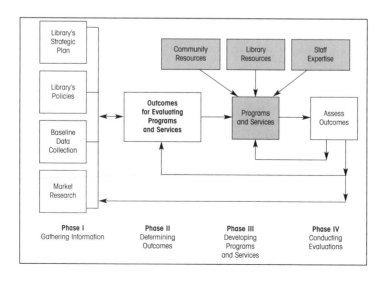

105

Using outcomes helps focus a library's traditional youth programs on young people's needs, on how they react and change by participating. Chapters 6 and 7 explained how to collect information, including various stakeholders' views about needs important for the library to address. Chapter 8 gave directions for setting outcome goals on the basis of the information collected. Chapter 9 is about using these outcomes to design and provide programs and services that will meet the stated outcome goals.

In choosing which programs to do or services to provide, librarians ensure that the programs and services offered actually address the outcome goals. To do this, staff need to identify the target audience and available resources both within the library and in partnerships in the community. Librarians then think about how individual programs and services can be brought together and coordinated within all the offerings in the youth services department to meet the outcome goals. By taking time to plan, librarians can design better programs with more positive impacts.

Using the Information Gathered

In the first phase of OBPE, information is assembled about the library, about the community, and from and about users. The point of collecting all this information is to use it to design programs and services that actually meet the needs of those using them. Articulating outcomes helps the library focus on particular impact goals. Each program or service must be planned to relate to the stated outcomes. Even programs that are fun, successful, and in demand can be adapted to relate to specific, identified outcomes. In fact, these solid field-tested programs may be the key to meeting stated outcomes successfully.

Because outcomes change from year to year, programs and services should also change from year to year. For example, if an intended outcome is that preschoolers attending storytime be able to play simple musical instruments, storytimes should include time for children to play music and learn more about it. Even if the storytime sessions in question have been well received without a musical component in the past, to meet the goal of building children's musical skill the sessions should be changed.

Not all storytimes are about music, and each kind of program is likely to be designed with several compatible outcomes in mind. Some other outcomes for storytime might be that children enjoy books (attitude), or learn how to sit still (skill), or attain readiness for school (status). Although there is a limit to the number of outcomes a program can address, library staff should make sure the program being produced meets the identified outcomes. This is fairly self-evident when the outcomes are specific and the programs are being modified rather than newly developed. But if a desired outcome is that students using the library improve academically, for example, it may be less obvious how the library can be successful. Actions can be on a grand scale, like adding staff to help with homework after school. Or they may be subtle, like providing quiet study areas (or listening stations, for students who study better with music).

Matching programs to outcomes is also more sophisticated than simply providing a program on the topic of the outcome. OBPE also demands that a successful program attract its target audience, that it be age- and skill-appropriate and interesting enough to hold the audience's attendance. Programs also have to be of high enough quality to benefit the children attending. Common sense dictates that programs and services be about appropriate topics or needs and well enough presented to attract and improve the children attending.

Selecting the Target Audience

After gathering information about the library, staff has to choose which groups to target for service. It is possible that outcomes are very focused and that the target audience is stated in the outcome. For Level I or Level II programs, the audience may be obvious, in which case the program planner need only make sure that the program is designed for that audience. If there is a larger potential audience than can be served, then youth services managers should identify audience subgroups and set priorities on who is to be served during the current planning cycle. If an outcome focuses on getting children ready for kindergarten, for example, the library has several choices. Possible audiences include preschool children, parents of preschoolers, preschool teachers, and kindergarten teachers. There may be specific subgroups within these audiences, such as young immigrant children, fathers of preschoolers, Head Start teachers, or first-year kindergarten teachers. Obviously, many other audience segments could be identified.

To select the target, library staff must determine which groups would benefit most from the service and which are most closely aligned to the stated outcomes. If an outcome relates to non-English-speaking children, it is logical to target immigrant families and the specific Head Start programs that serve them rather than all preschool children in the community. If the library's goal is to help parents get their child ready for middle school, the target might be all parents of fifth graders and each middle school principal. Selecting a target audience that most closely matches outcomes is the first step to planning a program that has a positive impact on those who attend.

Finding Library Resources

After determining which programs or services relate to the desired outcomes and selecting a target audience that will enhance efforts toward those outcomes, the next step is to identify the necessary resources. Normally this includes financial support, staff time and skills, facilities/space, collections, and volunteers, if appropriate. Special products or performers that are paid or donated are sometimes involved. Librarians are accustomed to working within a budget and getting the most out of their resources, but sometimes programs fall short because resources are not available to support attendees effectively.

The librarian's most immediate financial resources are within the library, whether through an annual program budget or one proposed for individual programs. But librarians should also consider seeking grants and donations to support outcome-based programs. As mentioned in chapter 2, foundations and other donors often appreciate outcome-based planning and are generous in support of these programs because they have clear goals and built-in evaluations. Librarians can also solicit volunteers and donation of in-kind gifts of products and services that support programs and services.

The next resource to assess is staffing available for specific programs or services. Some libraries have trouble finding staff time to prepare for and present yet another program. If this is the case, then to find a way to add or expand services and programs the youth services manager may have to offer an established program less often or eliminate programs that are less effective. Another staff consideration is the skills and knowledge needed to provide new programs. If a staff has all the skills necessary, then the planning can proceed, but if it lacks some essential skills then staff training must be part of the plan. A regular skill and interest survey of staff may uncover hidden strengths. Understanding that staff may lack familiarity or be uncomfortable with some target audiences helps plan training for the skills needed to be successful serving these groups.

Other necessary resources include library space appropriate for the intended programs and services and suitable collections, public computers, and the like. Is the picture book collection large and strong enough in books about starting school to support a pre-kindergarten program? Is there a comfortable and welcoming preschool area at the library where parents and children can read about going to school? If the library lacks some of the needed resources, it may be possible to meet at a school or share materials from other area libraries. Assessing library resources to shape the selected program improves the program, makes it easier to present, and brings all the available resources together to better reach outcome goals.

Finding Resources and Partners outside the Library

Some programs and services require partnerships and cooperation from other agencies. Often programs include schools, day-care centers, and other child-serving agencies as locations of programs or places to recruit participants. School partners may give teachers time to participate in library in-service training or advertise library programs to children or parents. Scout groups can bring children to the library or encourage them to use library resources on their own. Groups that serve older adults may arrange for members to tutor in the library after school.

Various arts or theater groups, including high school and college groups, may perform at the library or offer special performances at theaters or studios. Service groups may raise money or volunteer at children's programs. Local businesses may donate services or give discounts to the library. National or regional groups may also partner with the library to provide programs and services. The Red Cross may offer first-aid classes; a regional Hispanic group may sponsor a fiesta at the library where children can learn more about Hispanic culture. The library should have policies about appropriate partnerships. Many libraries require letters of agreement that describe what each partner will provide to avoid problems as work progresses.

To develop people and organizations as partners, the librarian needs to attend community meetings, work on community projects, and make needs known through the United Way and other community-based groups. It may take years to develop strong partnerships, but starting with simple projects may lead to larger support. Library administration and board members may also help open doors to partnerships in your community.

Coordinating Programs within the Library

Since libraries offer many different services, it is important to make sure that new or redesigned programs are a good "fit" in the library. This can be as simple as ensuring that new programs are not scheduled against other programs or a major busy service time. It may include pairing programs so that parents of children attending a library program can meet other parents or attend a parenting program all in one trip. New library programs can stretch the library to try new things and get new users, but this makes sense only if the library is ready to serve the target audience. If the library has no foreign language materials or non-English-speaking staff members, some preparation is needed before a major campaign to attract immigrant families should be implemented.

If an outcome-based project includes more than one activity or program, then coordinating the programs with other library events throughout the year is important. Coordinating departments to offer complementary programs and services can strengthen the program of each department. Programs done in the context of efforts of the whole library improve the chance of successfully achieving outcome goals.

One way to bring all these planning pieces together is to borrow from the field of marketing to organize the data gathered to help set priorities. In addition to using the Four Ps mentioned in chapter 6, certain market-defining questions can help the library describe its "brand," that is, who to serve and what to do to serve them:

- What business is the library in? (What is the library's role in this project?)
- What is the competition? (What other people or organizations offer services?)
- Who are the possible audiences? (Audiences could include children, parents, teachers, etc.)
- What is the primary consumer need? (What is the most important goal for our users?)
- What frustrations do our consumers have? (What makes it difficult to use the library?)
- What is our basic positioning? (What is the single most important reason someone would use the library?)
- What is the reason to believe in the library? (How will the library meet its goals?)
- What is our brand character? (What adjectives describe the library?) (Funosophy, unpublished report, 2002.)

Programs Designed to Achieve Outcomes

What follows are examples of bringing planning elements together to meet stated outcome objectives. In a Level I program, the St. Louis Public Library had the stated outcome objective of recording that 80 percent of elementary and middle school librarians use the library's databases through their school Internet services by the end of the current academic year. The library staff considered several possible programs and decided that the first step in getting schools to use its databases was to target school librarians. They also determined that it was appropriate to offer school librarians training, that the school was not able to offer this training, and that the most pressing need of the school librarians was to have hands-on experience with the databases. Library staff found out through focus groups and interviews that school librarians had trouble finding the databases from the library's web page and knowing which databases the library offered. Since the library offered many databases the school did not provide, staff decided that the library's resources would help schools provide students and teachers needed information. Since the library wanted to be known for its information and its helpfulness, staff offered workshops at the library computer lab for school librarians during their fall in-service day.

This program was a good "fit" because the library had a computer lab, staff who could provide instruction on using the library's databases, and a computer help line that could get school librarians started with the databases. Handouts and refreshments were paid for from the library's program budget. The school district partnered to give the school librarians paid time to attend the library workshop, and the school librarians signed a pledge to use a new database each month for the school year.

An example of planning for a Level II program is the development of a computer program for young teens. St. Louis Public Library staff developed the Club Tech program for middle school students. This was a redevelopment of an existing program. The original program, called the Computer Club, gave young people a chance to get together to learn more about computing. The children who participated enjoyed the experience, but turnout was low and staff had trouble providing activities that interested teens.

Because this program was not going as well as expected, the staff sought a grant to find out how to do a better job, and with funding from the IMLS Project CATE was born. Through CATE, staff heard from many children about what they wanted to learn and how the library could help. Children told staff that the Computer Club sounded dull and that they did not know what the club did. The Computer Club became Club Tech, and each week's program was described on flyers posted in the library. The grant paid a teacher to develop Club Tech activities and to train staff to direct them. Each session was evaluated by the teens attending, and these teens suggested topics for future programs, so the Club Tech sessions continued to evolve. Club Tech went to school. Library staff visited schools with computer labs and used Club Tech activities to improve students' and teachers' computer skills. Today, Club Tech continues to draw teens to the library and expand their computer knowledge.

Club Tech also benefited from the CATE OBPE model. Project CATE was developed as a major initiative to serve older children, particularly to help them better use computers. In the first phase, staff and consultants gathered information from and about children, their parents and teachers, and the community at large. This helped staff identify outcomes and plan programs. Using the marketing questions suggested above, the library set out to provide programs that would address the outcome goals.

An example using OBPE to solve problems identified by Project CATE stakeholders involved broadening the uses of library computers by older children. Children said they did not know addresses of good websites to visit or how to navigate the Internet. Parents and teachers expressed worries that children spent too much time playing on the computer, and that neither they nor the children knew how to find "better" sites. Everyone agreed that the library had a key role in causing positive change.

After gathering information on what children knew and what they wanted to know, staff concluded that the children had a limited knowledge of websites and limited skill at searching topics of interest. Children spent a majority of time at game sites, because these were the sites they could find.

Baseline research noted that children who computed at the St. Louis Public Library had to negotiate an adult environment and asked for more kid-appropriate sites and activities. Children said that one thing library staff could do was recommend good websites and make the web addresses available to them.

Staff saw several things that would help young people use a wider variety of websites. Club Tech and school outreach helped groups of children learn about a variety of specific activities they could do on the Internet. Staff recommended sites more often. Some locations posted "Website of the Week" on white boards in the computing area, websites were added to bibliographies and newsletters, and most locations organized sessions in which middle school students reviewed and recommended sites for children.

To make sure these activities were making a difference, library staff collected quarterly information on what children actually did on library computers. After the library's assistance, children selected a greater variety of websites, spent more time on research, and showed less interest in games, as observed and recorded by PDAs (table 9-1).

Another example from Project CATE that shows how setting outcome goals can improve library service is the initiative to help children make safe decisions

Table 9-1
St. Louis Public Library In-Library Computer Use

	2001	2003
Games	48%	33%
E-mail/Chat	3%	1%
Word Processing (e.g., typing handwritten reports)	11%	10%
Serious Work (catalog, databases, search engine)	24%	30%
Other (topical websites like PBS Kids or NBA.com)	14%	26%

when using the Internet. One-third of students indicated that they would give personal information to a stranger on the Internet or did not know what to do when asked for personal information. The library staff set the outcome goal that after one year fewer than 15 percent of students would give out personal information.

The library found many ways to communicate directly with children as well as parents about Internet safety. A letter about Internet safety given to parents was revised to be clearer, more specific, and easier to read. Specific safety information and activities were included in Club Tech. Staff was trained to remind students to take safety precautions when using library computers. When a second safety survey was taken the following year, fewer than 10 percent of students responded that they would give out personal information to a stranger on the Internet. About 60 percent of students now thought that they knew how to be safe on the Internet. More information on Project CATE can be found in appendix B.

■   ■   ■

Whether programs are individual, in a series, or part of a whole package of programs and services for several target audiences, matching programs closely to user needs and library outcome goals increases the impact of program participation. Phase III in OBPE program planning is like cooking a great meal. The program planner thinks about what children need and would enjoy and how all the program ingredients can be put together to create a delightful and fulfilling experience for them. Better planning produces better programs, and these better programs have greater impacts on those served.

Ten

Phase IV
Conducting Evaluations

Implementing programs and services is a rewarding aspect—perhaps the most rewarding—of the planning and evaluation process. Working with young teens on a website they are building for the child-care center next door, or interacting with infants and their caregivers in a lap-sit program, or participating in a poetry blast for middle schoolers, or dancing and singing with preschoolers at the end of a themed story hour, or helping a pregnant teen find community resources she needs all bring pleasure and a feeling of success.

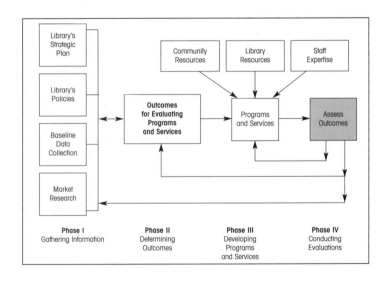

But Phase IV of the CATE OBPE model, evaluation, can be just as exciting. This rings true because evaluation tells the real outcome of all the library's effort, from the user's point of view. And if perchance things have not gone as well as they could have, evaluation is what keeps the programs and services on track; it is important to know if programs and services are having a negative outcome or falling short in some way, even though the hope is that all outcomes will be positive.

Evaluation simply means determining the significance or value of something through focused study. In the CATE OBPE model, it means finding out whether and to what extent the desired outcomes of a program or service have been accomplished. The evaluation must assess whether the desired outcome— be it a change of skill, knowledge, attitude, behavior, or status for the young people participating in the program or service—has occurred.

Instant Evaluation

Some evaluations occur at the moment a program or activity is taking place. "Instant" is a way to describe much early twenty-first-century communication. Communication via cell phone or instant messaging puts much of the world's population instantly in touch with someone possibly continents away. A flick of the TV switch brings on-the-scene news into homes, cars, or PDAs. So it only makes sense that librarians who work with youth want to know instantly the results of their efforts. Obviously, long-term outcomes cannot be known instantly, nor can the impact of multifaceted programs (Level III efforts), which require multifaceted evaluation. But if evaluation of a single program or activity not associated with a series of related programs is required, or of only one of a series of programs, instant evaluation of short-term outcomes is possible— and documentation of progress toward outcomes is easy.

Club Tech has been mentioned several times in this book as a Level II program of the larger Level III Project CATE effort. How Club Tech became an important program on the basis of Phase I data and how the outcomes were formulated from that data in Phase II are explained in chapter 9. But how successful was the program? It is important to remember in constructing even the simplest instant evaluation what outcome you are assessing, what indicators you are looking for, what your objectives are, and how you are going to measure those objectives. Five skill-based outcomes for Project CATE were targeted as part of Club Tech: basic computer skills, keyboarding, searching for information online, use of application software (Microsoft Word, PowerPoint, Excel), and creating websites. Since the young people in focus groups had expressed a strong desire to learn in a sharing and clublike atmosphere, Club Tech was created as a fun way to achieve the desired outcomes.

Two instant evaluations were conducted with Club Tech. One was carried out through observation by the staff working with the youth (see chapter 7 for considerations about evaluation through observation). The purpose of the observation was to note what changes in knowledge and skills the young participants exhibited for technology-related outcomes. The staff were familiar with the desired outcomes, so they were able to assess quickly whether the youth were achieving them. Even when there was no formal measurement such as a test or culminating exercise, the staff had indicators and objectives in mind. This made their observed evaluations easy. When the outcomes and indicators have been established before a program is planned, it does not require much time or effort for the staff to recognize whether the desired outcomes are reached. At the end of the program, the staff involved jotted down observations, which were shared at a weekly staff meeting. In a public library planned and recorded observation, guided by specific outcomes and outcome levels, is the most practical and prevalent type of instant evaluation. All library staff observe their young patrons, but without awareness of desired outcomes and indicators they often do not recognize and certainly do not record what they observe. This, again, is an advantage of the CATE OBPE model. It provides an accurate and instant way to evaluate the outcome of a program or activity, because the desired behavior, skill, or knowledge is anticipated, and it is easy to see if it has been achieved. Attitude and status cannot be as easily observed.

The other type of instant evaluation used for Club Tech came through participants' written input. Youth participating in each session were asked to fill out a brief three-question survey on their reactions to the activities of the day. How the Club Tech evaluations were used is discussed later in this chapter.

Various means can be used to collect on-the-spot data. An informal survey with only a few questions works well with middle elementary through high school students. Younger children can circle smiley faces or give other nonverbal representations of pleasure or displeasure. Many older children can articulate well in verbal responses.

One of the most effective means of determining the impact of programs and services on people's lives is through individual interviews. Sometimes these too can be "instant," although they often work best when planned in advance. Young people of all ages are often willing to talk about things that are important to them. Even preschoolers, when appropriate techniques are used, can provide valuable insights to program planners. For example, a social worker in Wisconsin used puppets to talk with young children (McDonald and Willett

1990). Another strategy with young children is to assume roles—for example, they can be the librarian and you the child. Rather than presenting interviews to young people as something formal and therefore scary, they should be billed and carried out as conversations or chats.

Instant evaluation can become as prevalent in public libraries working with youth as cell phones and instant messaging are in the lives of tech-savvy youth. It can become second nature to staff if outcomes, indicators, and objectives have been determined through the processes outlined in chapters 6–9. It is knowing in advance what to look for that makes the job easy. Staff, both professional and technical, in the St. Louis Public Library reported that knowledge of outcome levels that guided observation of and assistance for youth trying to reach them made their jobs easier and most enjoyable. The impact of what they were doing was crystal clear and, if the outcomes were not achieved, they knew that their programs and activities had to be changed.

Ongoing and At-the-End Evaluation

Formative and summative evaluation are formal types of evaluation. Formative evaluation is ongoing and occurs throughout a project. Summative evaluation takes place at the end of a project or at major stopping points.

Formative Evaluation

Instant evaluation is one kind of formative evaluation. It can shape and form the planning process even when it is still under way. Planning and evaluation were once seen as a linear (and then a circular) process. But just as the arrows on the CATE OBPE chart loop around and connect "Assess Outcomes" to all other phases, so evaluation is embedded throughout the process and can modify any part of the process as it occurs.

Other types of formative evaluation can be more formal than instant evaluation, such as when Project CATE focus groups were used to evaluate young people's perceptions of the degree to which programs and activities helped them achieve outcomes they desired. Skill in online searching was one of the outcome areas identified in Phase I of Project CATE. After a few weeks, users would not be completely competent, but applying the indicators for the levels of competence, young people as well as librarians could access for themselves the progress they were making. In cases where it was apparent that the young users' progress would not allow them to reach the objectives set in the time targeted, librarians had to reassess the programs and services in content and delivery or reassess their targets.

Formative evaluations are never considered final. They are never looked upon as a stopping place where decisions about continuing and ceasing a program or activity take place because the desired outcomes have or have not yet been achieved.

Summative Evaluation

An exciting aspect of learning OBPE as defined by the CATE OBPE model is that, when starting with Phase I, a program manager already knows how to gather the data needed for summative evaluation. A summative evaluation of outcomes is appropriate at the end of a multifaceted program. Consider an example in which data have been collected, outcomes established, and programs and activities planned and implemented for two new child-care centers in a low-income neighborhood near the library. After an agreed upon period of time, the library must engage stakeholders in a systematic and more comprehensive evaluation. The data collection instruments are the same as those used to collect baseline data and to elicit opinions from stakeholders about desired outcomes. But this time, rather than inquire about what outcomes should be accomplished, staff ask stakeholders about the extent to which the desired outcomes have been reached (and data to design new outcomes should be collected at the same time). Because baseline data were collected at the initiation of the planning and evaluation process, comparisons can be made with data collected as part of the summative evaluation.

As detailed in chapter 9, the recorded use of computers at the beginning of Project CATE was compared with the data collected two years later, after outcome development and program implementation had occurred. The statistics alone demonstrated that computer use had shifted from game playing to more serious web searching, something the young people themselves as well as other stakeholders had stated as a priority.

Up-Front Evaluation

One of the significant features of CATE OBPE referred to throughout this book is starting up front with stakeholders, getting an assessment from them about outcomes they desire, and developing outcomes, indicators, and measurements based on that information. Library staff, of course, are also stakeholders who have input along with community and participant stakeholders. Formative and summative evaluation are part of almost all evaluation systems; the emphasis on preplanning evaluation, setting outcomes up front with the help of stakeholder input, sets the CATE OBPE model apart and gives it much of its effectiveness.

Can the CATE OBPE Process Start Anywhere?

It may not always be possible to start a planning and evaluation process at the beginning, just as accessing outcomes does not always start at the end. You may want to use the CATE OBPE model to evaluate a program or activity already in progress. Or you may have initiated a program or activity without the opportunity to gather data from stakeholders.

Certainly you may start at any point with the CATE OBPE model. If you cannot take full advantage of planning up front, start where you are. Eventually you will "cycle back" and find that you are planning based on the desired outcomes of your constituents—as long you keep this goal in mind. Possibly you have done a needs assessment as part of strategic planning or even program planning. This differs from direct involvement of stakeholders in setting outcomes, but it helps direct the program toward user needs.

If a program is in progress, you might hold interviews or focus groups at the end to determine the outcomes, both current and desired. Then the process can be taken back to Phase II and the setting of outcomes for additional program and service plans. Most likely, unexpected outcomes will come up in end-of-program assessments. For example, in Project CATE no desire or need to develop an outcome regarding gender and computer use was articulated in the baseline data, focus groups, interviews, or surveys. We did notice, however, that what participants said about their perceptions of gender differences did not coincide with observed behaviors. This suggested the need for revisiting the outcomes to determine whether we had missed any factors related to gender that needed to be considered in program planning. Not all outcomes can be detected up front, but when they appear serendipitously they can be integrated into the process.

So, even if the evaluation process starts where it might normally stop (or where a decision might be made about stopping or continuing), OBPE should be moving toward eliciting desired outcomes from users and other stakeholders before the planning process begins as well as incorporating into planning any unexpected results. Ideally, with the CATE OBPE model, evaluation starts the minute planning begins.

What Happens to the Results of the Evaluations?

One of the most important features of the CATE OBPE model is its iterative and interactive application. Take a careful look at the CATE OBPE chart. The many arrows show that one phase affects other phases and brings up the topic of possible adjustment or rethinking of the phase affected. Note that assessing outcomes can bring about changes in information gathering (Phase I), outcome determination (Phase II), or program and service development (Phase III). Conversely, each of these phases affects the assessment of the outcomes (Phase IV).

To answer the question that heads this section, then, the results of up-front, formative, and summative evaluation, in-depth or instant, have the potential to effect changes in all other parts of the model application. The model is iterative (planning and evaluation happen repeatedly) and interactive (evaluation affects planning and planning affects evaluation continually and at all steps of the process). This section reviews just a few of the many illustrations of how up-front, formative, and summative evaluation, whether extensive or on-the-spot, can improve all aspects of the library, from the overall strategic plan and policies to the outcomes themselves and the programs and activities based on them.

Application of an Evaluation
Assessing Attitude

The baseline data gathered in the St. Louis Public Library demonstrated that the attitude of young users was extremely positive, so no desired outcomes in terms of attitude were formally set for the project. But other libraries, like some in which the ALSC preconference workshop participants worked (see Introduction), found attitude to be something that everyone involved, including the youth, wanted improved. A typical desired outcome might be that youth participating in programs or activities have a positive attitude toward the library and librarians. In this case, specific indicators would be developed, for example, that participants readily ask librarian's help with Web-searching activities. An objective could be that 100 percent of the young people who seem uncertain about searching the Web during a chosen week voluntarily ask the librarian for assistance—something leading to instant, on-the-spot evaluation. Or the objective could be lower initially, with higher expectations at each session; this kind of outcome should definitely have a summative evaluation that can be compared to the evaluation that showed the negative attitudes of youth in the beginning. After the intervention of a library program, attitudes should be more positive. If they are not, then the librarians need to return to the drawing board to rethink activities and approaches, and it may be necessary to give staff development sessions on interaction with young people. The point of this formative and summative evaluation is to know if the library's interventions are affecting attitude in the desired way.

Application of Results from Level I and Level II OBPE

The following examples provide an overview of the evaluation phase of the CATE OBPE model applied to specific programs and services. The two programs illustrated (in tables 10-1 and 10-2) were first encountered in chapter 4 (see tables 4-5 and 4-6). Notice that several categories have now been added to give a more complete illustration of topics explained in chapters 5–9: how outcomes are developed, indicators, objectives, methods of evaluation, results of evaluation, and, most important to Phase IV, application of evaluation results. How outcomes were developed is placed first in the new tables, since in chapter 4 we were not discussing the CATE OBPE model but rather demonstrating levels of OBPE programs or services selected for evaluation. Now that the use of the model has been explained, the examples in these tables could be laid out with the source of information first—always the ideal in using the CATE OBPE model to guide the process.

Note that tables 10-1 and 10-2 are designed to illustrate in detail the evaluation processes for outcomes at Levels I and II, with only scant information given about the other phases of the OBPE process and with a focus on how to apply the results. Reference is made to other model phases as they come up. Therefore, these tables are not intended to represent the entire CATE OBPE process.

In the table 10-1 example notice that, although the Level I desired outcome was reached and teens had become somewhat aware of the wide reach and futility of censorship, the librarians realized that much more work was needed for the young people to become both informed about and engaged by the concepts of intellectual freedom. The results of the evaluation were applied, and recommendations were made for changes in the strategic plan (Phase I) and in programs and services (Phase III). The results of evaluation are powerful in the OBPE model.

The series of programs characterized in table 10-2 constitute a Level II activity. Although each session was assessed (formative evaluation), an overall assessment was also conducted at the end of the series (summative evaluation). In this example, knowledge was the focus of the outcome. This program, as measured by the Web-based quiz, did not meet the desired outcome. However,

Table 10-1
Level I: Display with Specific Theme, Purpose (expanded)

How outcome was developed (source of information)	Teen advisory board members requested the display to make their peers realize the serious nature of censorship.
Desired outcome type	Attitude
Desired outcome	Young readers develop an appreciation for the wide reach and futility of censorship.
Level I program description	During Banned Books Week a display is placed at the entrance to the young adult section.
Effect on program planning	Incorporate some kind of activity, e.g., a large poster that asks those entering to make a comment about a banned book they have read. Consider how to encourage participation and what to do with requests to check out the books on display.
Methods of evaluation	Comment sheets ask young adults to list their name, age, and contact information if they are interested in joining a short teen focus group after Banned Books Week. If age is under 14, parent permission is required, per library policy. From the focus group results, the librarian selects various themes that might have an impact on future actions in the library and reads through all comment sheets. Finally she meets with the teen advisory board (TAB), which had suggested this type of display as needed and important.
Indicators	A good response to the activity, and comments from various sources that demonstrate surprise at the nature of book banning and note that it cannot succeed. It is not necessarily to devise basic, intermediate, and advanced indicators for this evaluation; this might more commonly occur with knowledge and skill outcomes.
Objectives	At least half of the young people who enter the young adult section during Banned Books Week fill out a comment sheet. At least 80% of the comment sheets and focus group members demonstrate surprise at the nature of book banning or note that it cannot succeed.
Evaluation results	Objectives were met and exceeded. From the focus groups, comment sheets, and TAB, the librarian concludes that the desired outcome was achieved. The TAB views the display as a success. Other teens are amazed that many of their favorite books, which ìcould not hurt anyone,î are included in the display. So they understand the widespread nature of censorship; they also note its futility, because if they could read these books, so must many other people. Several teens mention wanting to do something about spreading the word that good books are being censored.
Application of evaluation results	Librarians and TAB members realize how little the general young reader knows about censorship and recommend that action plans related to teens and censorship be included in the next revision of the strategic plan (Phase I), that the outcome retain its priority status, and that other activities be planned to achieve this outcome (Phase III).

Table 10-2

Level II: Series of Programs Celebrates a National Event (expanded)

How outcome was developed (source of information)	Librarians polled three classes of elementary school children in the targeted age range (fourth and fifth grade), their teachers, and several parents about what outcomes they would like to see from Black History Month activities. Almost all participants mentioned wanting to know more about the role of African Americans in the 1950s and 1960s.
Desired outcome type	Knowledge
Desired outcome	Children attending the programs know about African American history in the 1950s and 1960s.
Level II program description	For Black History Month, the children's room holds some activity each Saturday related to African American history. This series may be part of the library's general efforts to achieve the outcome of greater awareness and appreciation of library users for the contributions of persons from various racial or ethnic groups to American society. The children's librarian may be responsible only for planning and assessing the outcomes of this particular series of programs.
Effect on program planning	Decide which elements of this phase of history to include in the sessions and how to divide up the material among the sessions to achieve a satisfactory outcome.
Methods of evaluation	Web-based quiz in game form at end of each session and end of month. Informal chats with at least three participants to see what they learned.
Indicators	Children can respond accurately to questions about African Americans in this period of history.
Objectives	All children attending the program achieve at least 80% on quiz at end of each session and at least 70% on quiz at the end of the program.
Evaluation results	All children scored at least 50% on all quizzes, but objectives of 80% and 70% were not met. In informal chats, however, children articulated an excellent understanding of the contributions and tribulations of African Americans.
Application of evaluation results	Librarians use the results to examine the program content as well as the methods of evaluation. Perhaps the program could be presented in a more engaging fashion in another offering. Or perhaps the Web-based quizzes offered only factual information, and in such a short period of time the children gained more of an overall understanding. Librarians also reexamine the outcome, thinking the type of knowledge (specific factual or conceptual) might need to be specified. Another survey with young people could try to get at what it was they wanted to know. This evaluation did not call upon the staff to make recommendations on the strategic plan or library policies.

focus group data indicated that students knew more than the quizzes reflected. Thus the application of the evaluation information calls for some changes before this series of programs is offered again—changes in the type of outcome targeted or the assessment methodology, or perhaps a decision not to offer these programs again. Many different decisions might result from this assessment, but without the assessment librarians might have been satisfied that the desired outcome had been reached, never realizing that it had not.

Application of Results from a Level III OBPE

The evaluation of a multifaceted program is also multifaceted. Project CATE and other programs partially described in chapter 4 and displayed in tables 4-10 through 4-13 all require multifaceted assessment. The evaluation of such complex projects cannot be represented in tables such as those displayed above for Level I and Level II evaluations. Project CATE is the Level III program described here because the real results of the evaluation efforts are available (see appendix B for the final report on Project CATE).

APPLICATION OF ON-THE-SPOT EVALUATION

In Club Tech, on-the-spot evaluation occurred by observation of the participants throughout each of the ten sessions. Since each session resulted in products, evaluation of the competence of the participants on the tasks at hand could be assessed easily. If young participants were not achieving the desired outcomes, staff might give more assistance or otherwise alter the activities. Generally, the youth did well in achieving outcomes and meeting objectives, but on a few occasions the staff did make modifications in session content or methodology.

APPLICATION OF FORMATIVE EVALUATION

The following example describes an up-front impact of outcome assessment, something that affected policies in the St. Louis Public Library even before programs and services were developed. This assessment did not take place in Phase IV (Assessing Outcomes) but rather in Phase II (Developing Outcomes), and it brought about a change in Phase I.

When the data from the focus groups were examined in Phase II to develop the outcomes, it was clear that some outcomes young people wanted were being prevented by current St. Louis Public Library policies. Librarians realized, for example, that for youth in St. Louis computer use is not necessarily a solitary activity. In the focus groups, the young users revealed a strong desire to work with others on the computers and to share their knowledge. This resulted in a change to the library's "one person to a computer" policy and a rethinking of the physical arrangements of computers and chairs, which also worked to enforce this policy.

Another example of policy-related obstacles brought to light by analysis of the focus groups involved the policy requiring a library card for access to the computers. In this community there is a high level of in-library use of resources; some parents do not want their children to check out library materials and, therefore, to have library cards. But this self-imposed lack of borrowing privileges was also limiting access to library technology. Discussion resulted in the idea of issuing technology cards that would allow parents to authorize access to the computers without authorizing checkout—another policy change effected by an outcome assessment.

In neither of these cases did the entire process need to be complete for the library to consider a policy change. The policies were impeding the overall outcome of the project, which was to improve children's use of and access to computers, so the policies were changed. This type of interaction and application of results may occur throughout the CATE OBPE model's phases.

APPLICATION OF SUMMATIVE EVALUATION

Summative evaluation of a Phase III project must be multifaceted. The overall end-of-project results, in addition to the successful application of the model, are too complex to reproduce in full here, but two examples follow.

One important part of the summative evaluation of Project CATE outcomes was focus group interviews with top-level administrative staff. The director of neighborhood library services, the marketing director, the director of the central children's room, the directors of technology services (central and branch), and the director of the library were among those attending both an initial session at the beginning of Project CATE and a final session. Although the grant had ended, the St. Louis Public Library had determined to continue Project CATE with LSTA and local funds, so this assessment was important for continued improvement. But it was also important to the library in that the administrators saw applications for the model that went beyond technology and even beyond youth services. Some of this outcome assessment and how it was applied follows:

■ Branches that have not been involved in Project CATE are extremely anxious to be part of the project. They have seen the positive results. Overall, any services the project staff found successful, others will try to adopt.

- Library policies, for example, requiring individual use of computers have changed based on project results, and other policy changes are planned in the future.
- Needs of children and technology had previously been underestimated. The library now realizes that many kids are not getting adequate computer instruction or practice either at home or at school and are therefore depending on the library. Closer cooperation with schools will be a goal.
- The library website was little used and needed a major overhaul (which it received) to make it more appealing to youth.
- Library planners are much more aware of this age group than previously in planning and setting policies, and they act upon this awareness.
- With Project CATE training, the marketing department is much more aware of how to reach targeted user groups and has implemented what it has learned across the board. The result is that kids and the whole community are more informed about library programs and services and attendance and circulation have increased. The head of marketing said, "We were connecting with the outside world, but not the right part of the outside world. We now have ways of hitting those whom we serve. This started with kids but has gone way beyond."
- The head of technology services for the branches stated that the personal technical assistants (PTAs)—technical staff assigned to work with computers and users, particularly youth—have become more aware of the needs of young people and that the young people are more comfortable with them. These staff members have gained a greater understanding of adolescence—and of the nature of the relationship between adults and youth of this age. The project has changed what the library looks for in PTAs. It now looks much more for a "customer service" orientation and puts more effort into training the PTAs with the skills children need. The way PTAs assist the young people will be carried on.
- The director of neighborhood services observed that the Project CATE model would be used for services to seniors or other targeted groups.
- Library staff involved in Project CATE also participated in an end-of-project interview.

Here are some of their outcome assessments and applications:

- One of the most successful programs with young people was Club Tech, developed directly from desired outcomes for youth expressed by persons surveyed and in focus groups (parents, teachers, staff, and youth). This program attracted numerous young people and served as a magnet for other library services. One relatively new librarian said, "You can pick out who has been in Club Tech and who has not." Another staff member observed, "When kids ask you questions, you can tell they are really interested in what they are doing." Club Tech will be continued.

- Another positive outcome was improved library relationships with the schools, particularly the middle schools. As the head of the central children's services said, "Visits to the middle schools used to be a rare event; now they are routine. Teachers are shocked that we will actually come into the schools and do something." Middle schools visits and programs will be expanded.

- Project CATE has been about building relationships between staff members and young people—relationships that will endure long beyond the project. Young people have lost some of their reticence about talking with adults because of the surveys and focus groups. Librarians and PTAs feel much more accepted by youth and are approached more often. PTA assessment will continue.

The administration and staff interviews are only two small pieces of the evaluation of this multifaceted project. The final evaluation report of Project CATE was more than 100 pages long—much more than instant or on-the-spot evaluations but including many of them.

Sharing Results

The youth at the St. Louis Public Library let it be known that they enjoy learning in small groups, exchanging information about various library resources, and being part of a learning community. On occasion, adults in the library forget that they too are part of a professional learning community. OBPE is a new activity to everyone involved. It has not been on the library scene for long. So those who have successfully incorporated it into their daily lives must find ways to share their knowledge and the joys of knowing what the impact of library services are with colleagues and community.

The two common formal ways to disseminate information are through conferences and published articles. Both are appropriate means to share the results of projects that go beyond the commonplace. Usually those who become actively engaged in OBPE are so delighted with the process that they want to share their results. Many types of Internet venues—websites, blogs, chat rooms, e-mail—provide informal ways to share the results of projects. Librarians should take advantage of sharing results with all the learning communities to which they belong.

In the case of Project CATE, two kinds of results were interesting to professional colleagues—what we found out about children and technology and what we found out about OBPE. This book is about OBPE. But for those interested in more about Project CATE itself and youth and their technology use, read the summary end-of-project report in appendix B.

■   ■   ■

We hope you have found our roadmap through the CATE OBPE model easy to read and interesting to follow. We trust you have enjoyed the scenery (examples) along the way and now feel confident to begin, polish, or redirect your own OBPE process.

We have emphasized throughout that there are many individual choices to be made when applying the CATE OBPE model. The model's special iterative and interactive nature has deep consequences. It allows for quick and easy planning and evaluation or more comprehensive multifaceted processes. It acknowledges, however, that even Level I programs and services have effects on the larger library program and perhaps throughout the community as well. That is why it is so important to understand what changes in behavior, knowledge, skill, attitude, or status are generated by programs and services and how closely they match what stakeholders want from them.

There is, of course, an underlying motivation for the government's and local libraries' and librarians' interest in and commitment to OBPE. Behind this movement is the desire to make the most of products, programs, and services provided by "hitting home" with users. As far as possible within the vision, mission, and goals of the organization, libraries, like other agencies, strive to provide the positive results users themselves want and need. So once the pleasure of seeing positive change for young users is realized, OBPE will never be seen as a burden or just one more administrative task that diverts time and energy from direct service. Along with the staff of the St. Louis Public Library, we predict that if you use OBPE, you will soon be exhilarated because you will know that what you are doing has achieved its purpose—or you will be confident about what needs to be changed to best develop dynamic youth services. We hope that is the outcome of reading this book for you.

Sample Data Collection Instruments

Club Tech Survey

Location (circle one):   Buder   Julia   Davis   Gates Lab

Session (check one)

☐ Week 1: Learn to Keyboard
☐ Week 2: Create a Poster
☐ Week 3: Write a Review
☐ Week 4: Scavenger Hunt
☐ Week 5: Computer Music

☐ Week 6: Create a Web Page
☐ Week 7: Family Tree
☐ Week 8: All About Me
☐ Week 9: Graphing in Excel
☐ Week 10: Word Search

What grade are you in? (circle one)   5   6   7   8   9   10

How old are you? _____

How would you rate this program? (circle one)

    1   2   3   4   5   6   7   8   9   10
   bad   okay   good

I liked . . .	I didn't like . . .

Are you coming next week? (check one)   ☐ Yes   ☐ No   ☐ Maybe

Sample Project CATE Focus Group Question Guide
(for Students)

1. How often do you use computers and where?_____

_____

_____

Probes:

Do you use computers more or less at the public library than at school, home, or a friend's house? Why or why not?_____

_____

_____

2. How do you learn new things to do on computers? Does someone else show you how?_____

_____

_____

Probes:

What adults work with you when you are learning how to use computers? Does anyone at the public library teach you anything about computer use?

_____

_____

_____

Do you depend more on yourself, on friends, or on adults to learn how to do things on the computer? _____

_____

_____

3. What do you do when you use computers? Name as many things as you can think of. Talk about what you do most and least often._____

_____

_____

Probes:

Do you go to the same websites over and over? Why or why not?

_____

_____

_____

Do you use computers for school assignments, to find out things you want to know, or to play? _____

_____

_____

What do you like best about computers? _____

_____

_____

4. Do you think boys and girls use computers differently? If so, what do they do that is different? _____

_____

_____

Probes:

What do girls like to do on the computer? _____

_____

_____

What do boys like to do on the computer? _____

_____

_____

Project CATE Observation Guide

1. *Branch name.* The name of the branch in which data collection is taking place. Once the branch name has been selected from the list provided on the PDA, that name becomes the default selection for the day.
2. *Today's date.* The date (month, day, year) on which data collection is being performed. The first time this date appears, staff must verify that it is correct. After that, the date is automatically generated by the PDA.
3. *Staff name.* The name of the staff person collecting the data. The name is automatically generated after it is entered. When shifts change, the new staff person enters his or her name when they begin data collection.
4. *Computer type.* There are three types of computer stations available to users in each branch. These are "walk-up catalog," for which no appointment is necessary and the station's primary use is access to the electronic catalog; "walk-up reference," no appointment is needed and the station is meant for quick access to electronic reference sources; and "appointment computers," scheduled in one-hour segments and providing access to the library's full range of software as well as Internet access.
5. *Computer number.* Computers in the library are identified by an assigned number.
6. *Number of users at the computer.* This is a physical count of the number of users at a computer station.
7. *User's school grade.* This is taken from the sign-in sheet for appointment computers and estimated for users at walk-up computers.
8. *User's gender.* This information is recorded based on observation.
9. *User's race/ethnicity.* This information is recorded based on observation.
10. *Computer use.* Computer use is broken down into several fixed categories based on the types of resources the library provides. Categories include use of the St. Louis Public Library catalog, St. Louis Public Library web page, e-mail, computer game (Internet), computer game (CD-ROM), online subscription database (databases the library pays to access), search engine, chat room, other website, educational software (CD-ROM), and word processing. In addition to these fixed categories, an "other" category is available in case a user is observed accessing a resource that is not described by the preset categories.
11. *Describe other use.* When "other" is chosen in response to item 10 above, this field is displayed on the PDA and the person collecting the data provides a description, in their own words, of what the "other" use is. Although this did not happen often, other uses described by the data collectors include the use of typing software, use of clip art programs, and shopping on amazon.com.

Project CATE
Summary Report

Reducing the Digital Divide: An Outcome-Based Model
for Evaluating School-Age Children's Access
to and Use of Technology in an Urban Public Library

About Project CATE

Project CATE focused on the needs of fourth through eighth graders for library services in general and their needs for computer services offered at the St. Louis Public Library (SLPL). The project was funded by the Institute for Museum and Library Services (IMLS). Leslie Edmonds Holt, Director of Youth Services, St. Louis Public Library, and Eliza Dresang and Melissa Gross, Florida State University, conducted the project research. The project goals were to (1) gather information about the digital divide and describe how lack of access to computing affects children; (2) develop an outcome-based model for developing public library services to school-age children; and (3) develop programs and services that are effective and sustainable to serve older children. Research was conducted between February 2000 and February 2003.

Final Report

CATE research did identify and describe a digital divide that existed for St. Louis youth. Children in the study reported having limited access to computers in school and home and fewer computer skills and less knowledge of technology than reported nationally. Interest in computers was high, and computers were reported to be "cool" by youth and important by parents, teachers, and community leaders. All groups said that the library and library staff have an important role to help bridge the divide.

The SLPL serves 348,000 people with a central library and fourteen branches, an annual budget of $19 million, and 1,622,000 volumes with 34 circulations per registered borrower. The users are more than 50 percent minority, with 47 percent of those African American and 15 percent foreign born. St. Louis has about 88,000 children under the age of eighteen, and about 90 percent of them are considered to be "at-risk" (from low-income homes, parents with low levels of education, often from single-parent homes). Another challenge facing the city of St. Louis was the underachievement of students in the public school systems. In fall 2003, St. Louis pubic schools ranked 115 of 115 in the state and failed to meet state requirements for accreditation. Students were unable to perform adequately on skills tests given in spring 2002. The technology program at the SLPL is crucial for reducing the digital divide because its defined user community is urban, majority-minority, and includes many at-risk youth. The SLPL is within a context shared by other urban libraries.

The mission of the SLPL itself focused on improved outcomes, which positioned the administrators and board to adopt an outcome-based model for planning and evaluation willingly. CATE research informed program and service planning to offer more targeted activities for youth. The research offered a way to describe desired outcomes and suggested a line of study that would provide a mechanism to measure progress toward these outcomes.

General CATE findings

Almost all children were enthusiastic about computing and thought they were quite good at it, but in general their reported or demonstrated knowledge and skills were very limited. Almost all kids expressed the desire to gain more skills and knowledge.

Access to computers and the Internet varied from school to school but appeared to be limited overall, so access in the public library was considered very important by all stakeholders.

Kids tended to be very specific in their experience ("I have been at the PBSKIDS.org website") without having much of the "big picture" of the many ways computers could be useful to them.

Parents and teachers wanted assistance from the public library to help children have better computing experiences. Parents tended to understand that play and direct teaching are both important ways to learn, whereas teachers tended to think direct teaching only was essential. Parents were, however, often overly optimistic about their children's skills and knowledge, whereas teachers were generally pessimistic.

Specific Findings

1. Before Project CATE, the SLPL had little or no actual visibility in upper elementary and middle schools. Children were unaware of SLPL computer services, were not sure it was "cool" to use the library, and thought it was difficult to get access to SLPL computers.
2. Students literally made no mention of the SLPL website as an information resource.
3. SLPL computers were not used by a large percentage of children in the neighborhood. Smaller branches had a small group of users; regional branches had a somewhat more diverse user base. "Repeat" customers accounted for 32 percent of use.
4. At the beginning of Project CATE, 35 percent of computer work was serious (homework, catalog use, word processing), 51 percent was for recreation (games, e-mail, chat), and 14 percent was for other personal interests (non-homework websites).
5. Children ranged in ability but were generally unsophisticated, their knowledge narrow, and their ability to use search engines or to navigate limited. They were willing and interested in learning.
6. Parents and teachers knew very little about technology or children's use of technology.
7. Students had little knowledge of Internet safety, intellectual property, or information literacy. Teachers and parents were aware of the problem, but not of solutions.
8. SLPL staff help was highly valued by students, parents, and teachers.
9. Students expressed the desire to interact with others about computing—teaching older or younger people and sharing ideas with peers.
10. Kids who computed at the SLPL negotiated an adult environment and asked for more kid-appropriate sites and activities.
11. All participants showed great interest in SLPL non-computer activities. The community saw the library as an integrated environment with technology as well as other information sources and services.
12. Both boys and girls identified differences in computing by gender (boys play more games, girls use e-mail and chat), but these differences did not appear in our measures of actual use.

13. Kids, parents, teachers, and community leaders could articulate outcomes they wanted from children's use of computers in libraries. They did not, however, always agree.

In addition to using data and direction from users about technological services, Project CATE developed an interactive, outcome-based, transferable planning and evaluation model, and its use for improving technological services for youth was demonstrated at the SLPL. Best professional practices (programs and services) were devised on the basis of desired outcomes and implemented. Marketing strategies involving youth were initiated.

Because Project CATE was exploratory research, it raised as many questions as it answered. Project CATE results suggest that there are several myths about children and technology. For example, data collected challenge the ideas that children's affinity for computers makes them "computer wise," that gender differences in computer use are significant, and that computing is necessarily a solitary activity.

Unanticipated Results

As with many projects, there were some unanticipated results from Project CATE. Changes were made during the project in response to research results and to changes in resources and people available to us:

1. Because we could not find valid and reliable survey instruments to adapt, piloting survey questions and other data collection instruments took longer than anticipated, and results from data collection in the first year of the project (2001) were suggestive rather than definitive. The research team decided that the surveys and focus groups "worked" and produced many accurate indicators of attitudes, knowledge, skills, and behavior. We did decide, however, that the measurements were not totally reliable or valid and thus needed more development. Therefore, we did not use the data collected as a baseline measure and we did not try to compare the early data with data collected at the end of the project.
2. When the Association for Library Service to Children (ALSC) conference was scheduled for St. Louis in October 2002, the research team took the opportunity to offer a preconference on Project CATE and to use the attendees as a soft focus group to review the CATE model and findings. This seemed to give us a variety of reviewers, including leaders in the field of youth librarianship, and provided a way to disseminate CATE

results. The preconference was so popular that we had to turn people away at the door, so we had not one focus group but three, and we were asked to repeat the program at the ALA annual conference in summer 2003.

3. Because we have considerable data, many developing program and service activities, and ongoing data collection, analysis is not complete. Most aspects of Project CATE need to be further explored and tested. Further development and testing will continue beyond the life of the IMLS grant.

In addition to these findings, the Florida State University researchers added the following unanticipated results:

4. The collaborative effort between the Florida State University School of Information Studies and the St. Louis Public Library was successful. It is easy to propose a collaboration, but making one work operationally to the benefit of all involved was a much more difficult task. As evaluators, we were able to discuss and define our roles effectively with the library's executive director, library administration, and Project CATE staff. One of us was invited to give a presentation at the Association of Library and Information Science Education, January 2003, based on the positive outcome of this collaborative effort. Many library administrators are competent researchers, and we, as evaluators, have participated in professional practice and library administration, so we could "speak each other's language."

   Because of the ease of collaboration, we could concentrate on the work at hand and never had to worry that we were out of step with the needs of the library or purpose of the grant. This success revolved around the library administrators' skill as leaders among their staff and the respect the staff has for them; development of routine, systematic progress reports and defined communication channels (always copying each other and project leaders in St. Louis by e-mail); and continual revisiting of project objectives and movement toward accomplishing the defined outcomes. The IMLS staff was also extremely helpful when questions arose, and the workshop on outcome evaluation was useful.

5. There was professionalism and a commitment by the SLPL staff to be a learning community. We paid many trips to St. Louis and met with staff of many job descriptions (administrative, central project staff, building-level librarians, technology staff, public information staff) during our experience. In every staff position we found interest in the project and

commitment to it. We were never denied access to anyone or made to feel that we were imposing on anyone. Moreover, as the project progressed, the staff grew more and more enthusiastic about it and committed to it, coming up with ways to carry it beyond the original goals.

6. There were impacts from the project at the SLPL beyond the scope of Project CATE. We set out to evaluate how children ages nine through thirteen use technology in a public library setting and whether the presence of computers reduces the digital divide. We were astonished, therefore, when we discovered the by-product of our research—that as the SLPL staff were trained in and embraced the outcome-based evaluation model, the library began to (in the words of the SLPL executive director) "change its way of doing business." This idea of user outcomes spread far beyond the youth involved in Project CATE and began to affect planning and evaluation in the system as a whole. Library staff have found the model applicable to many other services and user groups.

7. The application and development of the Project CATE OBPE model was successful. This model was developed prior to the beginning of the project and at that time was theoretically a good model, but it had not been tested. The methodologies we proposed in applying it (surveys, focus groups, interviews, market research) all worked well—in combination. Involving the young people themselves in determining what outcomes they wanted was particularly successful. We found the model to be even more powerful than we had originally envisioned. Its interactivity and flexibility became apparent as we applied it, and we found ourselves "adding arrows" to model diagrams to represent this higher level of interactivity. It is truly a model of the twenty-first century.

8. There were unexpected findings about kids and technology. When we embarked on this project, there had been no systematic studies of kids and technology in public libraries. We did not have predetermined ideas about what we would discover, but we did know some of the "comment ideas" about the topic, such as that youth are inherently skilled at computer use and that gender makes an enormous difference in how young people approach and use computers. Neither of these preconceived notions held up in our research. The depth of the discussions in focus groups and other venues allowed us to make some tentative (and not previously discussed) assumptions about many areas of young people and technology. Our findings cannot be considered generalizable because the sample was not random and may not have been representative, but they are transferable to understanding young people in other communities and situations.

9. The technology program implementation was successful, and there was an interdependence of technology with other programming. We found that successful technology programs can be planned to help achieve desired outcomes, but we also found that technology is intricately intertwined with all public library services to youth and cannot be examined as a completely independent unit. The homework helpers, for example, proved to be extremely valuable technology assistants—and they were not built into the design. Offering other types of programs often led youth to an interest in technology. The learning environment was much more complex than originally anticipated.

10. The partnership with public schools was successful; it was extremely encouraging to see it grow and develop. Initially this relationship was a small component of the design. By the end, evaluating the success of the project had to include acknowledging the enormous improvement in communication with and partnership with the public schools, particularly at the middle school level.

11. There has been a keen interest in Project CATE from the professional and academic community. We have had many opportunities to speak to both professional and academic audiences. Each appearance seems to generate several more invitations for one or all of us. Researchers, state library officers, heads of children's services in large libraries, librarians in all types of libraries, and graduate students have all seemed attracted to and interested in our research results. We have had numerous opportunities to publish results of the project, have created a course that seems to have generated interest, and are continuing to disseminate our results.

Accomplishment of Project CATE Objectives

Goal 1: Train librarians; collect baseline and market research data (surveys, interviews, and focus groups)

At least one staff person from each CATE location attended monthly training meetings. Staff learned how to gather information using surveys and in-house interviewing techniques. These staff members also learned how focus groups are formed, and they contributed questions and review of the focus group content. New staff members were trained to collect, analyze, and understand data.

CATE activity staff developed survey instruments, piloted them, and instructed other library staff on how to collect data. Survey results were reported to unit youth services staff and to unit manager and SLPL administrators.

First-year research results were reported to staff in a series of meetings in January 2002.

Project staff developed the measurement instruments. CATE contracted with the marketing group Funosophy after contacting several specialists in the field of marketing to youth. Funosophy delivered its report, which included an assessment of SLPL current marketing efforts and a proposal for a CATE marketing campaign for the 2002/03 school year. Funosophy provided training on effective marketing techniques for staff in October 2002.

The initial surveys included approximately 100 parents and teachers, 100 children, and 25 community leaders. The adults and children reflected the demographics of St. Louis. Most of the children queried throughout the research were users of the SLPL, though some surveys were filled out by class groups that included both users and non-users.

During the second year of the project, shorter surveys were given to children. This reduced reading problems identified with the original surveys. Staff discussed the responses to these surveys and used them to target services to CATE-age students. For example, one survey asked middle school students how often they took care of younger children when they were at the library. Since about 40 percent of the middle school youth reported looking after young children, library staff began planning activities for the younger children during SLPL middle school programs so that the middle school caregivers would be free to participate in age-appropriate programs.

Goal 2: Develop CATE outcome-based model and refine using Delphi study

A draft of the CATE outcome-based model was developed but is not ready for a Delphi study. Project staff developed two models. One is a preliminary outcome-based service matrix based on Project CATE, and the other is a planning model. Because these models are drafts, a formal Delphi study would be premature. The models were vetted at a meeting held in conjunction with the ALSC national conference held in St. Louis in October 2002.

Goal 3: Train librarians. Develop, deliver, and evaluate the pilot trial interventions for the outcome-based children's technology program using CATE model

CATE programs were evaluated by participants, and the input from these evaluations was used to plan future programs. For example, Club Tech participants are asked what bored them in the program and what questions they would like answered in future programs. CATE staff used this information to plan the next session as well as the next Club Tech series.

Youth services staff had a list of topics presented in each Club Tech session so that they could reinforce participant learning. They also submitted topics for programs based on their conversations with young users.

Program descriptions and attendance from June through December 2000 (pre-CATE interventions) were collected. Beginning with June 2001, CATE programs were begun in six locations (since Carpenter branch was closed for renovation, its CATE services were all school-based). The 2001 programs represented more attention to services for fourth through eighth grades. Programs based on research results were offered beginning mid-2001.

CATE Activities

Club Tech. This program offered directed computer activities to middle school students as an ongoing after-school program. More formal computer instruction was developed as part of the SLPL FY2003 Institutional Plan and piloted with middle school class visits in fall 2003.

Middle school visits. Because middle school teachers indicated an interest in learning more about SLPL and using its services, CATE staff visited middle schools throughout the city. Staff visited teachers and offered programs to classes in spring and summer 2002. Fall visits are regularly scheduled. As a result, participation in summer reading club and attendance at CATE programs increased. Participation of middle school classrooms in summer reading club tripled in two years (2001–2003). Programs offered during the school year went from serving seven classes and about 150 students in 2001 to serving 125 classrooms and 2,500 students in 2003.

Cluster programs. CATE staff organized series of both paid and staff-produced programs, each offered at several locations. These attracted good audiences and were easier to market than individual programs. Several outside groups were identified as good presenters. Attendance at these programs doubled—most programs drew fifteen to twenty participants, and CATE programs are now being offered at all SLPL locations.

Individual computer advisory. In response to CATE research, staff tried to find ways to be more proactive in giving advice to youth about good websites and to give search advice when students are looking for particular information (similar to providing reader's advisory). Technology staff were trained to help youth expand their knowledge and skills, and all direct service staff were proactive in helping youth understand Internet safety and use a wider variety of websites. Many locations identified a new site each day for students to visit, and staff developed a location on the SLPL intranet to share good sites among staff.

Teen Zone web project. Many teens expressed interest in a teen location on the SLPL web page. A professional designer developed several web "looks" from which teens and staff selected elements to make the best teen page. A group of teens were solicited to be part of the Teen Zone staff and to create the complete teen web page; contribute articles, photos, and illustrations as well as links; and manage an ongoing opinion poll for web visitors.

Program Evaluation

The major tasks of this phase were to develop, deliver, and evaluate the pilot products and services that were trial interventions to improve the outcomes of children's access to and use of technology. All programs were evaluated by the participants and by library staff through regular monthly reports and program assessments done by the staff presenting the program. Staff met monthly to analyze the evaluation and initiate services and programs based on the evaluation. Thus the CATE model of getting continuous input from the users to improve services was implemented.

Because baseline measures raised questions about the effectiveness of the instruments, no major comparative community assessment was done at the end of the project. Because the marketing data were collected about a year into the project and implementation of marketing techniques was just beginning, there has not been replication of the marketing research. Specific marketing research for CATE-aged youth are being conducted in 2006.

Use statistics by CATE participants were collected and analyzed on an annual basis and recorded in the SLPL annual report as well as being sent to the Missouri State Library.

Staff at all levels recommended continuing Project CATE, providing CATE services at all SLPL locations, and continuing to use the CATE model as a planning strategy. The CATE model will be used to develop a literacy plan for SLPL (supported by LSTA funds). A library-wide marketing study was conducted to improve marketing to users of all ages. This study was inspired by the results of the CATE marketing study. A future project will develop techniques for measuring improvement of knowledge and skills of youth who use the library's computers.

Dissemination Activities

Before the completion of Project CATE, Dr. Leslie Holt spoke on CATE to staff at the Hennepin County (Minnesota) Public Library and the New Zealand Library Association's annual conference. Results of CATE research were used in a presentation for the Kansas City Public Library board in their discussion of computer policy for children.

Dissemination began as research was completed. A print instruction manual draft was developed. Dissemination of project findings and results have been submitted to library and information science and marketing periodicals for publication and presented at professional meetings. Project CATE staff and research will continue to seek opportunities to share CATE results.

Urban public library directors and coordinators of children's services in urban public libraries, state children's coordinators, and the Urban Library Council were informed of CATE findings. Youth librarians took the outcome-based course offered by the Florida State University School of Information Studies in the spring of 2004.

Sustainability

SLPL funded the Project CATE staff with library funds and is committed to continue to develop services for St. Louis youth. The Florida State University OBPE course will be repeated as long as there is interest at the modest continuing education fee.

When the CATE planning model, standards, and evaluation tools are fully developed, researchers plan to approach the ALA/ALSC with the CATE model for official adoption and dissemination through the association and profession with possible expansion to other aspects of children's programs in libraries.

Topics for Further Study

As researchers for Project CATE, we will continue to analyze the large amount of data collected, speak, and generate publications. We anticipate more opportunities as we teach the course on outcome evaluation generated by the project. Questions we posed for Project CATE will continue to be answered as we delve more deeply into data already collected but only partially analyzed. We expect to be able to make more statements about young people and computers and the digital divide after this further analysis.

The research team has proposed the following goals for further research:

Goal 1. Refine, enhance, and implement programming and services on the basis of user-desired outcomes for middle school students, their parents, and teachers and caregivers (with more focus on longitudinal studies of individual families).

Goal 2. Expand the interactive, adaptable, and sustainable Project CATE OBPE model.

Goal 3. Further develop and explore attributes of the internal and external learning communities supporting technology-related services at the SLPL.

Goal 4. Build a learning community of public libraries and research partners, led by the SLPL, selected to test and refine the expanded Project CATE model.

Goal 5. Develop collaboratively with local and national partners twenty-first-century standards or guidelines for planning, evaluating, and monitoring technology-related youth services in public libraries that assure competent, self-directed learners.

Goal 6. Validate or modify the Project CATE results-oriented planning process and technology-related learning standards in collaboration with national experts on youth services in libraries.

REFERENCES

Annie E. Casey Foundation. n. d. a. Kids Count census data online: 2000 census data: Race profile for St. Louis, Missouri. http://www.aecf.org/cgi-bin/aeccensus.cgi?action=profileresults&area=2965000P& areaparent=29S&printerfriendly=0&section=2.

_____. n. d. b. CLICKS, Community-Level Information on Kids: Profile for St. Louis, MO (county). http://www.aecf.org/cgi-bin/cliks.cgi? action=profile_results&subset=MO&areaid=116.

Babbie, Earl. 2004. *The practice of social research*. 10th ed. Belmont, CA: Wadsworth/Thompson Learning.

Bertot, John, and Charles R. McClure. 2003. Outcome assessment in the networked environment: Research questions, issues, considerations, and moving forward. *Library Trends* 51:590–613.

Bertot, John, Charles R. McClure, and Joe Ryan. 2000. *A guide for using statistics and performance measures: Public library networked services*. Chicago: American Library Association.

Bradburn, Frances Bryant. 1999. *Output measures for school library media programs*. New York: Neal-Schuman.

Case, Donald O. 2005. Principle of least effort. In *Theories of information behavior*, ed. Karen E. Fisher, Sanda Erdelez, and Lynne (E. F.) McKechnie. Medford, NJ: Information Today.

Chula Vista Public Library. 2005. http://www.chulavistalibrary.com/ About/mission.asp.

Dresang, Eliza T. 1990. Interviewing using micro-moments and backward chaining. In *Evaluation strategies and techniques for public library children's services: A sourcebook*, ed. Jane Robbins, Holly Willett, Mary Jane Wiseman, and Douglas L. Zweizig. Madison, WI: School of Library and Information Studies, University of Wisconsin–Madison.

Dresang, Eliza T., and Melissa Gross. 2001. Evaluating children's resources and services in a networked environment. In *Evaluating networked information services: Techniques, policy, and issues*, ed. Charles R. McClure and John C. Bertot. Medford, NJ: Information Today.

Dresang, Eliza T., Melissa Gross, and Leslie E. Holt. 2003. Project CATE: Using outcome measures to assess school-age children's use of technology in urban public libraries: A collaborative research process. *Library & Information Science Research* 25:19–42.

Druin, Allison. 2005. What children can teach us: Developing digital libraries for children with children. *Library Quarterly* 75:20–41.

Druin, Allison, Benjamin Bederson, Juan P. Hourcade, and Lisa P. Sherman. 2001. Designing a digital library for young children: An intergenerational partnership. In Proceedings of CAN/IEEE Joint Conference on Digital Libraries, Virginia, June.

Druin, Alison, Ann Carlson Weeks, Sheri Anita Massey, and Adrienne LeGier. 2005. International research with children: University of Maryland 2005. http://www.icdlbooks.org/research/imls.shtml.

Durrance, Joan C., and Karen E. Fisher. 2005. *How libraries and librarians help: A guide to identifying user-centered outcomes*. With contributions by Marian Bouch Hinton. Chicago: American Library Association.

Fiore, Carole D. 2005. *Fiore's summer library reading program handbook*. New York: Neal Schuman.

Funosophy Inc. 2002. Project CATE brand positioning. Unpublished report, St. Louis Public Library.

Glaser, Barney G., and Anselm L. Strauss. 1967. *The discovery of Grounded Theory: Strategies for qualitative research*. Chicago: Aldine.

Gross, Melissa, Eliza T. Dresang, and Leslie E. Holt. 2004. Children's in-library use of computers in an urban public library. *Library & Information Science Research* 26:311–227.

Himmel, Ethel, and William James Wilson. 1998. *Planning for results: A public library transformation process*. Chicago: American Library Association.

Hwalek, Melanie, Victoria Essenmacher, and Amy Juntunen. 2002. *Junior Girl Scout group experience outcome measurement guide.* New York: Girl Scouts of the USA and SPEC Associates.

IMLS Institute of Museum and Library Services. 2002. Frequently asked OBE questions. http://www.imls.gov/grants/current/cmt_outcomes.htm.

Jefferson City News Tribune Online Edition. 2000. Public Schools in St. Louis make improvements in test scores. November 27. http://newstribune.com/stories/112700/sta_1127000026.asp.

Jue, Dean K., Christine M. Koontz, and Keith Curry Lance. 2001. Collecting detailed in-library usage data in the U.S. public libraries: The methodology, the results, and the impact. Paper presented at Third Northumbria International Conference on Performance Measurement in Libraries and Information Services, Newcastle, UK.

Koontz, Christie M., Dean K. Jue, and Keith Curry Lance. 2005. Neighborhood-based in-library use performance measures for public libraries: A nationwide study of majority–minority and majority white/low income markets using personal digital data collectors. *Library & Information Science Research* 27:28–50.

Krejcie, Robert V., and Baryle W. Morgan. 1970. Table for determining sample size in a given population. *Educational and Psychological Measurement* 30:608.

Lancaster, F. W. 1977. *The measurement and evaluation of library services.* Washington, DC: Information Resources Press.

Lee, Deborah. 2003. Marketing research: Laying the marketing foundation. *Library Administration & Management* 17:186–88.

Lévesque, Jeri. 1999. *St. Louis Public Library Project REAL final report.* Washington, DC: U.S. Department of Education.

McClure, Charles R., Amy Owen, Douglas L. Zweizig, Mary Jo Lynch, and Nancy A. Van House. 1987. *A planning and roles setting manual for public libraries: A manual of options and procedures.* Chicago: American Library Association.

McDonald, Lynn, and Holly Willett. 1990. Interviewing young children. In *Evaluation strategies and techniques for public library children's services: A sourcebook,* ed. Jane Robbins, Holly Willett, Mary Jane Wiseman, and Douglas L. Zweizig. Madison, WI: School of Library and Information Studies, University of Wisconsin–Madison.

McNeal, James U. 1999. *The kids market: Myths and realities.* New York: Paramount Market Publishing.

Mellon, Constance Ann. 1990. *Naturalistic inquiry for library science: Methods and applications for research, evaluation, and teaching.* Westport, CT: Greenwood Press.

Miles, Matthew B., and A. Michael Huberman. 1994. *Qualitative data analysis: An expanded sourcebook.* 2d ed. Thousand Oaks, CA: Sage.

Missouri Department of Elementary and Secondary Education. 2002. 2001 Missouri School District computing census. http://www.dese.state.mo.us/schooldata/four/115115/map7none.html.

Nelson, Sandra. 2001. *The new planning for results: A streamlined approach.* Chicago: American Library Association.

Nelson, Sandra, and June Garcia. 2003. *Creating policies for results.* Chicago: American Library Association.

Powell, Ronald R., and Lynn Silipigni Connaway. 2004. *Basic research methods for librarians.* 4th ed. Westport, CT: Libraries Unlimited.

Robbins, Jane, Holly Willett, Mary Jane Wiseman, and Douglas L. Zweizig, eds. 1990. *Evaluation strategies and techniques for public library children's services: A sourcebook.* Madison, WI: School of Library and Information Studies, University of Wisconsin–Madison.

Rudd, Peggy D. n. d. Documenting the difference: Demonstrating the value of libraries through outcome measurement. In *Perspectives on outcome based evaluation in libraries and museums.* Washington, DC: Institute of Library and Museum Services. http://www.imls.gov/pubs/pdf/pubobe .pdf.

St. Louis Public Library. Mission, Goals, and Governance. http://www.slpl .lib.mo.us/using/mission.htm.

St. Louis Public Schools. Accreditation. http://www.slps.org/Acred .Strategies/accred.htm (accessed March 6, 2003; page now discontinued).

Schalock, Robert L. 2001. *Outcome-based evaluation.* 2d. ed. New York: Kluwer Academic Press.

Siegel, David L., Timothy J. Coffey, and Gregory Livingston. 2001. *The great tween buying machine.* Ithaca, NY: Paramount Market Publishing.

Spielberger, Julie, Carol Horton, Lisa Michels, and Robert Halpern. 2004. *New on the shelf: Teens in the library. Findings from the evaluation of public libraries as partners in youth development, an initiative of the*

Wallace Foundation. Chicago: Chapin Hall Center for Children at the University of Chicago.

United Way of America. 1996. Measuring program outcomes: A practical approach. http://national.unitedway.org/outcomes/resources/mpo/.

————. 2003. Outcome measurement in national health & human service and accrediting organizations. http://www.unitedway.org.

U.S. Congress. 1993. *The Government Performance and Results Act of 1993.* 103d Congress. http://www.phaseonecg.com/referencedocs/legislation/Government%20Performance%20Results%20Act%20of%201993.pdf.

Walter, Virginia A. 1992. *Output measures for public library service to children: A manual of standardized procedures.* Chicago: American Library Association.

————. 1995. *Output measures and more: Planning and evaluating public library services for young adults.* Chicago: American Library Association.

————. 2001. *Children & libraries: Getting it right.* Chicago: American Library Association.

Weber, Robert P. 1990. *Basic content analysis.* 2d ed. Newbury Park, CA: Sage.

Yohalem, Nicole, and Karen Pittman. 2003. *Public libraries as partners in youth development: Lessons and voices from the field.* Washington, DC: Forum for Youth Investment with the Urban Libraries Council.

Zollo, Peter. 1999. *Wise up to teens: Insights into marketing and advertising to teenagers.* 2d ed. Ithaca, NY: New Strategist Publications.

INDEX

Eliza T. Dresang, the Eliza Atkins Gleason Professor in the Florida State University College of Information, received her Ph.D. from the University of Wisconsin–Madison. Her research and teaching focus on information behavior of youth and leadership of adults in public and school libraries. Her publications include *Radical Change: Books for Youth in a Digital Age and School Censorship in the 21st Century*. She has served on ALA Council and on the boards of the Laura Bush Foundation for America's Libraries, the Freedom to Read Foundation, and the Association for Library Service to Children (ALSC); and she has chaired the ALSC Newbery, Batchelder, Belpré, and Research Committees.

Melissa Gross is Association Professor in the College of Information at the Florida State University. She received her Ph.D. in Library and Information Science from the University of California, Los Angeles, in 1998; received the prestigious American Association of University Women Recognition Award for Emerging Scholars in 2001; and has published extensively in the areas of information-seeking behavior and library program and service evaluation. Dr. Gross has a special interest in children as a user group. Her most recent book, *Studying Children's Questions: Imposed and Self-Generated Information Seeking at School*, was published by Scarecrow Press in 2006.

Leslie Edmonds Holt consults with libraries and child-serving agencies. She was the Director of Youth Services at the St. Louis Public Library from 1990 to 2004. She taught at the Graduate School of Library and Information Science at the University of Illinois–Champaign. Dr. Holt was president of the Association for Library Service to Children (ALSC). She received the Carroll Preston Baber Award from the American Library Association to support her research on how children use library catalogs. She has done research on how to improve service to middle school students that is the basis for this book.